T0280969

Product Management Essentials

Tools and Techniques for Becoming an
Effective Technical Product Manager

Aswin Pranam

Apress®

Product Management Essentials

Aswin Pranam
Santa Clara, California, USA

ISBN-13 (pbk): 978-1-4842-3302-3   ISBN-13 (electronic): 978-1-4842-3303-0
https://doi.org/10.1007/978-1-4842-3303-0

Library of Congress Control Number: 2017962635

Copyright © 2018 by Aswin Pranam

This work is subject to copyright. All rights are reserved by the Publisher, whether the whole or part of the material is concerned, specifically the rights of translation, reprinting, reuse of illustrations, recitation, broadcasting, reproduction on microfilms or in any other physical way, and transmission or information storage and retrieval, electronic adaptation, computer software, or by similar or dissimilar methodology now known or hereafter developed.

Trademarked names, logos, and images may appear in this book. Rather than use a trademark symbol with every occurrence of a trademarked name, logo, or image we use the names, logos, and images only in an editorial fashion and to the benefit of the trademark owner, with no intention of infringement of the trademark.

The use in this publication of trade names, trademarks, service marks, and similar terms, even if they are not identified as such, is not to be taken as an expression of opinion as to whether or not they are subject to proprietary rights.

While the advice and information in this book are believed to be true and accurate at the date of publication, neither the authors nor the editors nor the publisher can accept any legal responsibility for any errors or omissions that may be made. The publisher makes no warranty, express or implied, with respect to the material contained herein.

Cover image by Freepik (`www.freepik.com`)

Managing Director: Welmoed Spahr
Editorial Director: Todd Green
Acquisitions Editor: Nikhil Karkal
Development Editor: Matthew Moodie
Technical Reviewer: Bob Monroe and Tathagat Varma
Coordinating Editor: Prachi Deshpande
Copy Editor: Lori Lynn Cavanaugh

Distributed to the book trade worldwide by Springer Science+Business Media New York, 233 Spring Street, 6th Floor, New York, NY 10013. Phone 1-800-SPRINGER, fax (201) 348-4505, e-mail `orders-ny@springer-sbm.com`, or visit `www.springeronline.com`. Apress Media, LLC is a California LLC and the sole member (owner) is Springer Science + Business Media Finance Inc (SSBM Finance Inc). SSBM Finance Inc is a **Delaware** corporation.

For information on translations, please e-mail `rights@apress.com`, or visit `http://www.apress.com/rights-permissions`.

Apress titles may be purchased in bulk for academic, corporate, or promotional use. eBook versions and licenses are also available for most titles. For more information, reference our Print and eBook Bulk Sales web page at `http://www.apress.com/bulk-sales`.

Any source code or other supplementary material referenced by the author in this book is available to readers on GitHub via the book's product page, located at `www.apress.com/978-1-4842-3302-3`. For more detailed information, please visit `http://www.apress.com/source-code`.

Printed on acid-free paper

Dedicated to Ram, Priya, Abhijit, Rex, and the Waterford collective

Contents

About the Author

Aswin Pranam is a product manager, ex-software engineer, and avid technologist. Prior to his current role as a senior product manager in a venture group at a top-tier management consulting firm, Aswin spent time working in technical roles at Google, Boeing, Disney, and IBM. Aswin has a Bachelor of Science in Informatics (HCI) from the University of Washington, a Master of Science in Information Systems Engineering from Johns Hopkins University and an MBA from Carnegie Mellon University. In his free time, Aswin is the founder of elixirlabs.org, a non-profit organization dedicated to building technical infrastructure for NGOs and resource-constrained organizations. To get in touch, please send an email to contact@aswinpranam.com.

About the Technical Reviewer

Bob Monroe is an Associate Teaching Professor of Business Technologies and the Co-Director of the MS in Product Management Program at Carnegie Mellon University. His work at Carnegie Mellon focuses on developing and launching new educational programs to teach the next generation of technology and business leaders how to do great things.

Prior to joining the faculty at Carnegie Mellon, Dr. Monroe designed and developed a wide variety of software products for companies including FreeMarkets, IBM, Carnegie Group, and OptiMetrics. Dr. Monroe holds a Ph.D. in Computer Science from Carnegie Mellon University and a B.S. in Philosophy and Computer Science from the University of Michigan.

Disclaimer

All views expressed in this publication represent those of the author and do not reflect in any way those of associated organizations, institutions, or groups.

Foreword: Product Management Essentials

Over the course of their careers, many people wonder how they might become a product manager. Perhaps they're a marketing analyst who would like to have more influence in deciding what products her company will build and sell, a software engineer who wants to work more closely with his company's customers, or a recent MBA graduate who is trying to find the best way to make her mark in the tech industry.

Whatever your reason for wanting to learn to be an effective product manager, this book can help you towards that goal. It provides a step-by-step, chapter-by-chapter overview of the broad array of skills and habits you will need to excel in the role. You'll explore the technical foundations underpinning internet-based applications, the basics of data management and analytics, and user experience design principles. Perhaps more importantly, you will also hear great advice from leading high-tech product management experts who are out working every day to bring great products to market.

There are, of course, a lot of skills that you'll need to learn to become an expert product manager and it will take more than reading a single book to master them all. But you have in your hands a roadmap and starting point for that journey, and a guide in Aswin Pranam who knows what it takes to succeed as a Product Manager. So read on, take notes, learn from the experts sharing their wisdom in interviews and interludes. The best way to get started on your path to becoming a product manager is, well, to get started. Take what you learn here and apply it to the project you're working on now. And then do it again. With careful study of these principles and deliberate practice, you'll soon become the expert product manager that your organization needs to bring great things to market. Here is where you start.

Bob Monroe, Associate Teaching Professor and co-Director, MS in Product Management Program at Carnegie Mellon University

Acknowledgments

I would be remiss if I didn't acknowledge all of the wonderful people who made this book possible. From direct / indirect content contributions, to late-night motivational calls, to providing inspiration / support / friendship on a daily basis, I truly appreciate everything all of you have done to add a fingerprint to this final publication.

Thank you.

Ram Pranam
Priya Pranam
Abhijit Pranam
Bob Monroe
Umesh Unnikrishnan
Sean Ammirati
Leslie Shelton
Romy Macasieb
Daniel Csonth
Amelia Crook
Grant Small
Sulman Haque
Ariv Adiaman
Raghav Nair
Arun Adiaman
Vivek Bhupatiraju
Kasim Siddiqui
Teja Katta
Karisma Desai
Omi Iyamu
Joseph "Big Joe" Greco
Karthik Bhupatiraju
Christian Hahn
Adharsh Ranganathan
Arko Banik
Nikhil, Matthew, Prachi, Sanchita, and all the good people at Apress.

Honorable mentions to instant coffee, 24-hour hackerspaces, hip-hop, and Google Docs.

Introduction

Product Management Essentials aims to condense all of the techniques, teachings, tools, and methodologies required to be an effective first-time product manager into a simple, digestible read. Over the past decade, the demand for technically-capable PMs who can interface with management, stakeholders, customers, and the engineering team has skyrocketed. In fact, top business schools like Harvard, Cornell, and Carnegie Mellon have begun integrating product management courses into their MBA curriculum (or creating dedicated product management degree programs). Although the market requires more product-minded individuals, most people have no insight into the product role, and the position is ambiguously defined to outsiders. The overarching goal of this book is to help you understand the product manager role, give you concrete examples of what a product manager does, and build the foundational skillset that will gear you towards a career in product management.

Goals:
Describe the roles and responsibilities of a product manager
Understand the skills and qualifications necessary to transition into a product role
Break down the technical, business, and design knowledge required to be an effective product manager.
Provide feedback and Q&A-style advice from top-tier product managers in the industry.

The primary audience of Product Management Essentials are individuals who are eyeing a transition into a PM role, or have just entered a PM role at a new organization for the first time. They currently hold positions as a software engineer, marketing manager, UX designer, or data analyst and want to move away from a feature-focused view to a high-level strategic view of the product vision. This publication is an all-in-one cookbook that covers the required foundational learnings to succeed as a product manager, and allows you to get a big picture understanding of the goals and expectations of a product lead.

PART I

■ ■ ■

Introduction: Getting Started

CHAPTER 1

▓ ▓ ▓

Introduction

"Any sufficiently advanced technology is indistinguishable from magic."

—Arthur C. Clarke

Back in the early years, smack dab in the middle of my undergraduate studies at the University of Washington, I was unmotivated, lackadaisical, and uninspired by my general course list. Physics. Chemistry. Philosophy. Dinosaurs (yes, dinosaurs). The classes came and went, and none of the subjects captured my interest, or managed to convince me to formally sign away my remaining two years of dedicated focus. One day, as I was munching on a stale cinnamon roll and frantically trying to sign up for courses after sleeping through pre-registration, my friend sat down across from me and inquired about the level of stress visibly present on my face. We chatted about my difficulty in finding a topic that I connected with on a deeper level, and I had just about given up for the day until she said softly "why not computer or information science?" Full of ignorance and a false sense of understanding, I fired back with a hint of brashness: "you mean troubleshooting technical issues and plugging in ethernet cords? No thanks." She laughed, shrugged off the sharp response, and proceeded to educate me for the next ten minutes about the power of product development, and the potential it had to change the state of the world. An architecture major, she likened software products as the virtual equivalent of constructing real-life dreamscapes with a blueprint, tools, materials, and labor. After ten minutes of drawn-out lecture, I decided to give in and slotted myself into an introductory computer science course. Hell, why not? The other majors weren't clicking for me, so I had nothing to lose in this temporary pivot. Little did I know, those ten weeks to come would spark the drive I was desperately searching for, and completely immerse me into the challenging world of technological innovation and product creation.

Fast forward half a decade, and the technology industry is booming now more than ever. Students and aspiring technologists alike are ditching the traditional high-prestige titles of "investment banker" and "management consultant" to join the ranks of startups and established tech behemoths, all with the intention of adding their digital fingerprints to a piece of tech history. Empires are being built almost overnight, and company valuations have ballooned to heights the world has never seen. Perhaps the most compelling argument to be made for working in tech industry is the raw ability to create and deploy products that millions of people can use in a matter of minutes. Couple that with the growing demand for software engineers, product managers, and technical staff, and you quickly begin to realize that the opportunities are endless.

That's where this book comes in.

The past few years have given rise to a relatively new role in technology: the product manager. Understandably, this creates a bit of confusion for practitioners who have become accustomed to titles like project manager, program manager, engineering manager, and so on. What's the difference? Isn't the product manager just a glorified idea guy? Is the PM part of the formal management team? What does a product manager actually DO? Over the course of the next couple hundred pages or so, I'll attempt to break down the PM role, provide real-life examples of PMs and their daily set of duties, and dissect the three

© Aswin Pranam 2018
A. Pranam, *Product Management Essentials*, https://doi.org/10.1007/978-1-4842-3303-0_1

main knowledge areas that make up the ideal product manager (technical, design, and product/business strategy). Everything will be explained from a ground-up, basic principles view, and I will attempt to trim the fat and avoid the fluff as much as possible. In the end, I want this to serve as a handbook for any new or aspiring PM to kickstart their journey and lay the foundation for their career in product.

And with that, let's begin.

What are the learning goals for this book?

At a high level, this handbook is meant to act as a primer for anyone interested in product management and strategy. Whether you're a software engineer, first-time entrepreneur, or experience designer, the book will tackle the following areas of development in detail:

Technical Foundations

- The web software stack

  Dive into standard web technologies (HTML, CSS, Javascript) and describe their role in building web apps. Also, touch on the front-end / back-end paradigm.

- Mechanics of the internet

  Trace the route of a typical web request, and describe the technologies touched before content is served on the browser (DNS, CDN, load balancers, etc.).

- SQL

  Spend time learning about the fundamentals of SQL, and why it is critical as a PM to know how to issue queries to a relational (or noSQL) database.

- Data analytics

  Data is a PMs best friend, and being aware of the current tools on the market and how to use them effectively will come in handy. We will take a bird's-eye view of the current products PMs use to make informed decisions.

- Software Development Life Cycle (SDLC)

  Walk through the differences between waterfall and agile (SCRUM) methodologies, and the typical process for running a development sprint.

- System Design

  Deconstruct system design questions and increase awareness of the components that make up a typical tech product.

Design Foundations

- Low-fidelity / High-fidelity wireframes

  Develop wireframes with Balsamiq and brainstorm best practices in UI design

- UI mocks & rapid prototyping

  Develop a rough, fleshed-out user interface for a mobile app using Sketch

- UX techniques

  Cover the advantages of user research, storyboarding, diary studies, etc.

- Design in everyday life

  Examine good design from bad design. Learn to spot the differences between a product that is intuitive for the user versus a product that needs improvement.

Product / Business Strategy Foundations

- Product vision

  Develop a product roadmap, product requirements document (PRD), and go-to market strategy.

- Leadership

  Learn to negotiate your views, lead without authority, and gain the respect of the development team.

- Product release

  Touch on the post-launch phases and dealing with the aftermath of a product that is pushed into the wild.

Small Steps to Mastery

As you can see, we're ambitiously trying to cover a ton of knowledge areas in the span of just a few hundred pages. Just remember: the goal here is breadth, not depth. You won't magically become technical by reading through the technical foundations section, nor will you have all the design knowledge required to become a product designer overnight. Each section (and subsection) listed in the contents can be covered extensively on its own, but we will skim over the basics in a noncomprehensive fashion. I'll give you enough awareness and savvy to be dangerous as a product manager, but I leave it to you to further explore these areas at the conclusion of this book. If you're keen on continuing your technical journey and becoming the best technical product manager on the planet, by all means continue. Likewise, if design is your passion, fool around with Sketch, Photoshop, and InVision on your own time and explore what the tools can do for you. The best teacher is experience, and you'll be infinitely more prepared if you apply the skills you develop in this process and supplement your learning by building your own products, attending meetups, and networking at conferences.

Lastly, please skip around if you're already an expert in one of the foundational areas. Software engineers will not benefit from spending time in technical foundations, so fast forward to design and product/business strategy to save yourself time and effort. The foundational areas are meant to educate those who are new to that particular vertical, so jump around at your own discretion. For new entrants into the tech industry, welcome, and read all the way through!

What the %&!# is product management?

When I'm at a bar and the conversation of career choice inevitably comes up when chatting with a new acquaintance, the back-and-forth usually goes as follows:

Them: So what do you do?

Me: I'm a product manager

Them: Oh, what's that?

Me: I'm responsible for a portfolio of products and held accountable for the vision, roadmap, and probability of success around what the team builds

Them: So do you code?

Me: Well…I did in a past life, but now I focus on higher level decision making. Usually around how the products are designed.

Them: Oh, so you're a designer?

Me: Eh….no. We have UI/UX designers for that

Them: Got it. So you essentially have to convince engineers, designers, analysts, and business development to get behind your vision and respect your input, with zero direct authority over their day-to-day, and build a successful, complete product that satisfies all of the needs of the end user?

Me: EXACTLY!

At least that's what I wish happened at the end of the conversation. Usually, I end up telling them I'm a project manager (a role they're familiar with) and keep the conversation moving. Regardless, the sentiment stands: a product manager is the linchpin that holds the moving pieces together. If the product is a major hit, the team gets the credit. If the product dies as soon as it's shipped, the product manager usually takes the blame. A good PM understands the complexity of juggling the interests of distributed teams, and sources input from every single stakeholder to guarantee the best possible outcome.

In order to dig deeper into the archetype of a PM, let's look at what real job postings for product manager roles ask for and tease out the similarities. Take a look at the descriptions below and try to notice overlaps in skill set.

PRODUCT MANAGER @ GOOGLE

- BA/BS degree in Computer Science, related technical field or equivalent practical experience.

- 4 years of product management or product design experience

- Product design experience, including in collaboration with stakeholders across internal and external organizations.

- Entrepreneurial drive and demonstrated ability to achieve stretch goals in an innovative and fast-paced environment

- Demonstrated ability to gather user requirements across diverse functional areas and convert them into a compelling product vision

PRODUCT MANAGER @ FACEBOOK

- 5+ years product management or product design experience
- Organizational and analytical skills
- 5+ years of experience in technical architecture of web applications and/or media products.
- 5+ years experience designing user interfaces
- 5+ years experience creating examples through wireframes and mockups

PRODUCT MANAGER, INSPIRE @ AIRBNB

- Product management leadership in the consumer internet space
- Experience Design centered approach. Candidates should have personalization, dynamic content, discovery experience
- Success developing products from concept to launch
- Incorporated data/insights into the user experience
- Ability to interact with, present to, and distill feedback from stakeholders of varying backgrounds
- Extremely capable communicator at all levels across all disciplines, clear presenter

PRODUCT MANAGER, MAPS @ UBER

- A computer science undergraduate degree or equivalent plus hands-on software engineering experience. Technical understanding should go from the highest abstractions down to the metal
- 2–5 years experience delivering highly successful and innovative consumer Internet products with your fingerprints all over them. You're very proud of what you've accomplished
- Stellar design instincts and product taste
- A high bar across the board, from your own contributions to the people you work with to the products you work on
- Finger-tippiness with data: you just go get the data you need with no muss/fuss and can whip it into an insightful story with no help. You know how to leverage data to make decisions without getting stuck in analysis paralysis.
- A never-ending desire to grow and learn.

Based on the job descriptions, do you notice any patterns? A lot of you may be wondering: where's the mention of agile? Why is there no mention of knowledge related to methodologies and development processes? If you're included in this vein of thinking, you're identifying qualities that are closely associated with a "project manager" role at high-tech companies. Granted, knowing the inner workings of an agile environment is necessary for a product manager as well, but that alone won't get you in the door.

If you distill the core requirements for a product manager into a set of terms based on the listings above, the overlaps that are most likely to surface are technical, design, data, user/customer experience, and strategy. No PMP, Scrum Master, or Agile certification necessary. Instead of settling on a process-focused view, the PM needs to be creative, flexible, and product-centric. Anyone can learn the ins-and-outs of running a successful sprint after they're hired into the company (or by reading a textbook), but the other skills in a PM toolset take much longer to develop.

Project vs. program vs. product management

To further drive home the differences between a product manager and project / program manager, refer to Table 1-1. In a nutshell, a **project manager** role is task oriented and delivery minded, a **program manager** role is technically centered and implementation heavy, and a **product manager** role is aggressively strategic and long-term focused.

Table 1-1. *Project vs. Program vs. Product Management*

Product Manager	Project Manager	Program Manager
- Responsible for the success / failure of product	- Responsible for on-time delivery and tracking of a project	- Responsible for implementation and technical decisions
- Often referred to as the "CEO of the product"	- Ability to execute and influence the timelines	- Ownership over a set of projects in some organizations
- Voice of the customer	- Breaks down milestones into manageable tasks	- Works in tandem with engineering and often runs the daily sprints
- High-level vision setting and feature development	- Operations-focused	

■ **Note** Due to the rising popularity of the product manager role, companies have begun to re-label traditional project or program manager titles to product manager to generate interest. Be sure to ask questions, read the description, and uncover whether the role is truly focused on the product-level duties.

The big fundamentals

Tim Duncan was one of the most prolific power forwards in the history of professional basketball. Nicknamed "the big fundamental," Duncan adopted a style of play that the majority of fans would classify as boring or monotonous. Duncan would either float near the basket and execute a turnaround hook shot, step back for the classic bank shot off the backboard, or simply lay it up if he could shake the defenders. Throughout his career, Duncan followed the same basic formula, over and over again, and ended up as a hall-of-fame caliber athlete.

Why am I telling you this? To drive home the point that fundamentals are everything, in basketball and in technology. If you exercise the part of your mind that gives you a competitive advantage over the competition, you distance yourself far away from the rest of the pack. Our approach will be to introduce the three pillars of product management and set the introductory seeds in your mind so they grow over time. The sharpest PMs who I've personally had the pleasure of working with have a potent mix of each individual area of study: technical, design, and product / business strategy. This doesn't mean you need to transform yourself into a rockstar software engineer or UX designer to succeed as a PM, but building awareness of the terminology and raw concepts can go a long way in a conference room.

Technical Foundations - A PM is tasked with creating a tech product that produces a solution to a problem that currently exists. If you view your product as a black box that magically functions because your engineers are talented, it removes you from discussion about tradeoffs, technical capabilities, and the state of tech advancement. At a basic level, we will cover how common technologies work and cover principles of software development.

Design Foundations - Just as important as the tech itself, the user experience and design of the product needs to be distinctive. Why is Uber so successful when taxis were readily available to the masses? Because it enabled the user to call a car, set a destination, and pay for the service in an effortless and intuitive way. Design is rapidly shifting from being a brief afterthought in the product timeline to placing itself at the forefront of product success, so learning how to test the experience with users and crafting a plan for designing solutions that work as intended should be part of the core ethos of every product manager.

Product / Business Strategy - Great PMs have foresight into the future that isn't immediately clear to the rest of the world. Everyone can spot current market trends and tell you "what's hot" this year, but what about the next three, five, or ten years? Putting together a complete roadmap, requirements document, and business strategy is mandatory for any PM, so we'll dig into the best practices for drafting up these artifacts as the book naturally progresses.

CHAPTER 2

∎ ∎ ∎

Guiding Principles

"Congratulations! On behalf of FutureTech Labs, we are delighted to confirm your offer to join our team as a Product Manager. We look forward to hearing your decision soon...."

After months of heads-down study, carefully honing your craft in dimly lit coffee shops or co-working spaces, and guzzling five-hour energy drinks, you've finally secured a role at the company of your dreams. After a brief orientation period, you receive your top-of-the-line, fully loaded Macbook on your first day at work, with a shiny employee badge with the title "product manager" superimposed over a less-than-flattering headshot taken of yourself weeks prior. You feel energized, proud, and ready to execute on your Steve Jobs-style vision to elevate the organization to heights it has never seen. In your first 100 days, you focus on setting up one-on-ones with engineering and design teams, introducing yourself to leadership and executive management, and drafting up a strategy for the next year and beyond.

Six months later, the dream suddenly becomes a nightmare. Your enthusiasm and false sense of pride will transform into a vicious cycle of feeling defeated, stressed, and frustrated by the lack of movement. The initial product roadmap you developed was detailed down to a T, but the engineering team hasn't bought into your goals, and you've failed to make any significant progress. Leadership is pissed, and your confidence is at an all-time low.

If the picture I'm painting seems bleak and hopeless, then I've done my job of alerting you early as to what happens when you don't follow the guiding principles of product management. If you walk away with anything from this book, I want you to remember the five basic principles that could make or break your introductory role in product management. From the day you sign on the dotted line of the employment contract, your presence is instrumental in the success of the team. Often, capable PMs fail early because they don't recognize the core principles of their field, and misinterpret the expectations leadership has set for them. Let's dive into the five cardinal rules of product management and break them down in understandable terms. Accept them as dogma early, and you're immediately in a headspace that prepares you to tackle any issue, technical or political, that presents itself in the work environment you're thrust into.

Kill your ego

A product manager has an enormous amount of responsibility, sometimes more so than other roles within an organization. However, the inflated sense of purpose and pressure can lead to negative consequences, including feeding directly into a personal sense of ego. A product manager that views himself/herself on a pedestal when compared to his or her peers is losing sight of the goal of building an incredible product. A raging god-complex isn't the least bit productive, and humbling yourself from time to time can foster the growth of a cooperative, collaborative environment.

© Aswin Pranam 2018
A. Pranam, *Product Management Essentials*, https://doi.org/10.1007/978-1-4842-3303-0_2

You're not the expert

As much as the PM is the "CEO of the product," it doesn't issue you carte blanche authority over every layer of the product, both architecturally and design-wise. If a conversation arises around the tech stack that should be used, loop in the tech lead / CTO. For tasks involving user experience flow design or UI frame mock ups, bring in the designer. Trust your teams to be experts in their particular area, and argue back only if you have data, evidence, or intuition about a user's needs to support your claim. Stepping on the toes of the engineering, design, or business team is the quickest path to alienating yourself, so understand your unique value-add to the team and play your position. The only exception to this rule exists in startupland if a company isn't able to hire a dedicated tech lead, designer, or business strategist, so the PM (with relevant background experience) plays more than one role simultaneously.

Make decisions

The tech industry moves at light speed, and waits for no one. A fresh hire PM may be overwhelmed with the number of decisions that need their green light, and can fall victim to analysis paralysis if too much time is dedicated to overthinking simple choices. If you're writing five-paragraph essays for emails that only require a one sentence approval, you're wasting time for both people across the wire. Whether you're supporting your decisions with blind intuition, empirical data, or team buy-in, the PM has to take the reins and exercise good judgement to keep the chains moving. Don't slow down the timeline bickering over minor details. Find a method to understand the order in which decisions need to be made. Insignificant tasks (e.g., wording on landing page, stock image selection) can be deferred, whereas strongly linked action items need immediate attention to prevent a sequence of events from being delayed. For complex decisions, set up a dedicated time to mull over the details and come to a conclusion. Time is a luxury you cannot afford to waste as a PM, so learn to consider the opportunity cost of each hour you spend on the clock.

Become comfortable with ambiguity

If there's one word that perfectly encapsulates the standard product manager experience, it's ambiguity. A PM's personal task plan is rarely ever set in stone, and you must embrace the feeling of being lost in the water. It's OK to be uncomfortable, restless, and anxious. A lot can change over the course of a product development timeline, especially if you're dealing with multi-year projects, so learn to adapt early and remain flexible enough in strategy and mentality to deal with unexpected curve balls that will be thrown at you over time. An average PM looks to his or her manager to ask what needs to be done; a great PM decides what needs to be done and looks to his or her superior to request the resources needed to execute.

Ask the right questions

Time is a non-renewable resource, and people don't enjoy wasting it, especially in a work setting. If you're in a meeting, user research interview, or client feedback session, it's imperative that the questions you ask are clear, concise, and generate useful insight that can be looped back into product development planning at a later stage. Asking an effective question is comparable to drilling for oil; if you do your research, prepare, and drill in the right spot, your yield will be high and effort will have paid off. If you follow a strategy in which thoughts are disorganized and you start breaking ground in random places, you're likely to waste time and walk away feeling distressed (with a bunch of empty holes on the ground). Think deeply about the objective beforehand, and understand that the "right" question posed to another individual can make or break the interaction from a product value perspective.

CHAPTER 3

■ ■ ■

The End-to-End Product Journey

"If you don't know where you're going, any road will get you there"

—Lewis Carroll

The **Software Development Life Cycle** (SDLC) describes the process for planning, designing, engineering, and releasing a software product or service. SDLC doesn't exist to prescribe a strict process for building products, but rather illustrates a logical sequence of events that need to take place in order for a product to be considered done. As we'll see later on, an iterative approach is ideal for software development when compared with a fixed, linear timeline. SDLC is widely understood and studied by major organizations as a top-level framework, and is split into six model phases (see Figure 3-1).

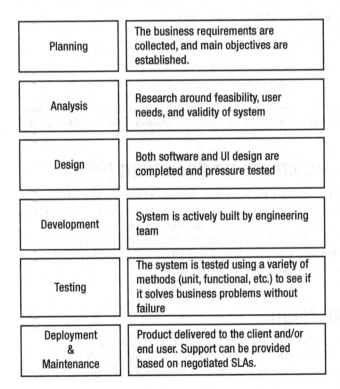

Planning	The business requirements are collected, and main objectives are established.
Analysis	Research around feasibility, user needs, and validity of system
Design	Both software and UI design are completed and pressure tested
Development	System is actively built by engineering team
Testing	The system is tested using a variety of methods (unit, functional, etc.) to see if it solves business problems without failure
Deployment & Maintenance	Product delivered to the client and/or end user. Support can be provided based on negotiated SLAs.

Figure 3-1. *The Six Model Phases*

© Aswin Pranam 2018
A. Pranam, *Product Management Essentials*, https://doi.org/10.1007/978-1-4842-3303-0_3

Being aware of the traditional SDLC concept is useful for a product manager, but the linear nature of the phases don't lend themselves well to describing iterative software development (covered in a later chapter). Instead, we'll step through an unstructured set of principles to keep in mind when going from product inception to polished end result that is consistent with the way products are developed at top-tier startups and tech firms.

Step 1: Ideation

Believe it or not, the idea is the simplest part of this entire journey. How many people do you know that utter the following phrase from time to time?

"I had the idea for [insert innovative product here] first. I should have followed through"

Before Uber existed, TaxiMagic and Hailo did the exact same thing. Instacart and AmazonFresh had a predecessor called WebVan that raised close to $400 million, but went bankrupt trying to do the same thing. The idea is just 1% of the equation; it doesn't go anywhere without a ton of strategy, luck, focused decision-making, legwork, and clear execution that comes after it.

That said, if the core idea isn't sound, it dooms the product (or startup) from the onset. An "Uber for Nachos" is a ridiculously dumb service, and there's no amount of execution or capital in the world that can make it a success. When brainstorming new products to build, ask yourself the following questions:

- Is it useful?

- Does the world need this product?

- Does this product exist in the market already?

- If it exists, can we launch a version which is a 10x improvement?

- Is it feasible in terms of cost, time, and resources?

- Does it solve an existing problem?

- Why hasn't the problem been solved already?

Everything you build should serve a purpose and alleviate the problem a user (consumer or enterprise) is facing. Otherwise, the product will end up quickly forgotten in the software graveyard shortly after launch.

Step 2: Create a product requirements document (PRD)

Once you have an idea, put it down on paper by creating a PRD. We'll go through a PRD and how to create one in detail during the product strategy chapter, but in essence, it's a document that describes the product, all of the features & requirements, and key details (timelines, risks, and so on). Start it off with a mission statement or core objective, follow up with the internals of the product, and finish with how you plan to execute on the vision. If the PRD is less than ten pages, it may not be thorough enough, so add as much detail as you can so all of the obvious questions anyone can ask are answered.

Step 3: Assemble the right team

Technical talent is underrated. Regardless of the salaries you see on Glassdoor or the fancy perks you hear about, people still treat engineers as an expendable resource. I can't tell you how many times I've been to a tech mixer and hopeful entrepreneurs go around asking for free labor in exchange for 5 percent of their company, which is nothing more than an idea.

When assembling a team, align incentives. Everyone wants something at the end of the day: money, recognition, prestige, equity, and so on. If you're a solo founder, find team members who are just as passionate about building something from the ground up. If you're a product manager at a major organization, round up members who want to start a new business line and eject themselves from a team that incrementally moves the needle each year.

Tips for team dynamics

- Never prioritize talent over ego. No matter how skilled, ego will ruin the flow of the entire team.

- Establish credibility. People will be drawn to your team if they feel like you're the right one to steer the ship.

- Be fair. Give credit where credit is due, and don't overinflate your contribution.

- Have a diverse mix of skills, backgrounds, and viewpoints.

- Establish ground rules, set up one-on-ones, and allow room for team members to air their thoughts and concerns on a monthly basis.

Step 4: Create a Minimum Viable Product (MVP)

Software isn't cheap to build if you're working with a team of experienced developers. Costs can easily cross over the million-dollar threshold if it's a technically complex product, so finding cheap ways to confirm that users want the product before investing all the chips at once is a smart thing to do.

That's where MVPs come in. An MVP is a proof-of-concept first version of the product that doesn't contain every feature on the wish list, but has enough functionality to be useable. For example, if you're building a massively multiplayer video game, build just one world first and test with users before developing the others. Or, if you're building a robot that delivers toothbrushes and toiletries to customers in a hotel, have one of your team members dress up in a convincing robot costume and have them deliver the item to the user. This may sound like a joke, but Star Wars has been using a human being to play R2-D2 instead of a mechanical robot, and Kenny Baker has done a pretty convincing job so far of making you believe it's a real robot, right?

The user doesn't know what's missing and what's been done intentionally. Using a bit of smoke and mirrors is okay if it prevents you from moving forward with a product nobody will use. In this phase, collect feedback from the user on the MVP, and note any changes, suggestions, or pain points that are immediately recognized.

Step 5: Establish product-market fit

Product-market fit, according to Marc Andreessen, means "being in a good market with a product that can satisfy that market." In other words, find a market that's sizeable enough to be interesting, then find the right product to disrupt the market. The easiest way to establish product-market fit is to rely on traditional metrics of success (revenue, user base, engagement, etc.), but what if you have a product that is still in the early stages?

Instead of using indicators or metrics that only come once the product is already successful, you can get creative with your approach.

Examples:

- Enterprise: for internal products, use a newsletter or group alias to drum up interest. Communicate the value proposition, then collect emails for follow up.

- Startup: create visual media and spin up a campaign on a crowdfunding website. If you can get orders before the product is fleshed out in the form of pre-orders, you'll prove there's a market for it.

The key takeaway from all of this is "don't solve problems that don't exist."

Step 6: Don't discount design

Design is a major driver of cash flow, but it's often an afterthought in development environments. UX / UI designers are an additional expense to a team, and costs are cut in the design department to focus more on pumping out functionality. To illustrate the importance of design, let's look at Hotel Tonight. As profiled in Fast Co. Design, Hotel Tonight was able to drive revenues up more than 10 percent by changing a simple confirmation logo. 10 percent! Users were accidentally booking non-refundable hotel rooms because their finger would slip and hit submit, and this resulted in a high cost to Hotel Tonight since they had to process a wave of customer service requests to correct the mistake on the side of the user. To remedy this, they decided to change to a checkout flow that involved the user tracing their finger over Hotel Tonight's iconic bed logo. In this design, there is no possible way a user can accidentally book a room, and it saved Hotel Tonight time and customer service resources. Not to mention a sizeable annual revenue bump. Design is critical; treat it as such.

Step 7: Source feedback

The voice of the customer is always available to you in the form of feedback, but it's a challenge to find the right way to capture it. As a product manager, you have to ask the right questions to mine the valuable info that can be fed back into the product. Surveys are a quick and dirty way to cast a wide net, but context is missed since you can't ask follow-up questions in real time. Interviews are better, but they require a time tradeoff. Find the correct balance that works for you, and use the feedback to continue meeting the user's needs. Problems and objectives can change over time, and becoming comfortable with the product at a fixed stage in its lifecycle is not a mindset that will lead to longevity.

Sample Q's for the user

- What problem does this product solve?

- Do you use any other products along with this one to accomplish the same task?

- What can be improved? What is the product missing in your opinion?

- What would cause you to stop using the product?

- Is the product easy to use?

- What are the key strengths of the product?

- Would you recommend the product to others? Why or why not?

Step 8: Obsess over metrics

Track everything. Collect every shred of data that passes through your systems, then recognize the patterns that'll lead to useful insights. A ton of users can tell you directly that they love your product, but if your monthly active user count is low, then the data tells a different story. Use the numbers from logs and analytics tools to corroborate the stories told by users in surveys or vocal feedback sessions. If there's misalignment, then you've found the disconnect that needs further investigation.

Step 9: Win or Learn

After the end of all the steps, the product can still fail. You could develop an MVP and drum up support, only to be crushed when the final version is out on the market. Factors out of your control can cause the product to slip, but how you react and learn from the experience is completely within your control. If mistakes were made along the way, find ways to self-correct and adjust. If bad team members were chosen, make a mental note and promise never to repeat the same mistake. Everyone will have a bad product or two in their career. Whenever this is the case, spot the holes in the previous game plan and come back with the lessons next time around.

■ ■ ■

CHAPTER 4

Industry Spotlight: Q&A with Umesh Unnikrishnan

Umesh Unnikrishnan is Head of Product Management, Search Ads at Pinterest. Prior to Pinterest, Umesh led product teams at Google (AdWords, DoubleClick, Wallet) and Microsoft (Office & Visual Studio).

What does the term "product manager" mean to you?

To me, a Product Manager "owns" the product end to end. Some companies actually use the title "Product Owner" for this role. As a Product Manager, your goal is to ensure the success of the product in all its dimensions. Your job is to get your users and customers to love the product, to enable the product to become a successful, sustainable business, and to make sure that the teams that work on the product are excited by the work they do.

What interested you initially about product management?

My first job out of school was as a developer on the Outlook team at Microsoft. I loved the work I did there - I got to build features that were used by millions of users and as a geek that loved network protocols and file formats, I got to spend a lot of time analyzing, debugging, and fixing related issues deep in the bowels of that product.

The first time I got to meet a real live customer though, I realized that users didn't care as much as I did about file formats and protocols, but cared more about what the product was doing for them and how it was solving their business needs.

That inspired me to get a deeper understanding of what business problems our products solved and how users were using them on a day to day basis. I realized that the most successful products, whether consumer or enterprise, were the ones that were solving real user problems in the simplest way possible. If you aren't solving a problem in the simplest way possible, someone else will come along and solve it better, taking your users and customers with them.

How do you deal with failure as a PM?

The default state of any product is failure. As a product manager, you need to create a path to success and remove the roadblocks that block that path. This doesn't guarantee success, of course, and when you eventually fail, you need to look back and understand the factors that caused the failure.

© Aswin Pranam 2018
A. Pranam, *Product Management Essentials*, https://doi.org/10.1007/978-1-4842-3303-0_4

Was it poor product-market fit or poor execution (or both)? Could more resources have solved the execution failure? Was the product too early or too late to market? Was the niche too small or the competition too intense?

Understand the reasons your product failed (and remember, the product failed, not you!). Do a post mortem of what, if anything, you could have done differently to change the outcome and either share it with your team or keep it to yourself depending on the culture and temperament of your organization.

Once you've internalized what happened and what you could have done differently, take a break and move on to your next project. A good PM has a long list of projects they want to actualize.

What tools help make your life easier as a PM?

As a PM, you'll be bombarded with requests every hour and your todo list is always growing. Have a system to tame and track that list. I'm personally a fan of David Allen's Getting Things Done methodology. I use Evernote to keep a log of everything incoming and then use a block of time at the end of the day to either do, delegate, or delete these todos. The more you keep off your mind, the more bandwidth you have to think, plan, and be creative.

How is product management different between enterprise and consumer products?

The biggest difference between a consumer product and an enterprise product is that for consumer products, the user and customer are the same person whereas for enterprise products the user and the customer are different people often with different motivations.

Consumers make the decision to buy, install, or use your product based on emotional reasons - is your product useful? Is it fun to use? Is it cool to use it? Does my peer group like the product and so on?

On the other hand, enterprises make purchase decisions based on business and political reasons. Is your product going to make or save us money? Is the product easy to deploy and support? Will I get fired or promoted for choosing this product?

Once you internalize this difference, it becomes easier to know who to build your products for and what to prioritize when building the product. You can make the easiest to use enterprise product with the sexiest UI, but if it's a pain to deploy and manage, no enterprise will buy your product.

PART II

Technical Foundations

CHAPTER 5

■ ■ ■

Understand the software stack

"Truth can only be found in one place: the code"

—Robert C. Martin

This will be the most ambitious chapter in the entire book. I'll attempt to walk you through a common technical product manager interview question that will give you insight into the way the Internet works, then cover the elements of a website to show you all the web technologies that play a part in the page being loaded in your browser. You will not magically become a web developer or immediately understand the nitty gritty of networking, but with additional study you will be able to firmly grasp the concepts we cover. If you already have a background in software development, skip past this chapter and move onward.

Why cover web instead of other technologies?

We're deeply rooted in the age of web and mobile development, and this will stay true for at least the next decade. More users around the globe are able to get online, and this opens up access to applications and experiences they weren't previously able to participate in. In addition, engineers are able to spin up web apps and build upon Internet technologies at a faster rate than ever, so it's a stable jumping off point as a first introduction. Lastly, coding bootcamps, both domestic and international, are focusing on training web engineers, since one can be brought up to an intermediate level of ability in a relatively short period of time (4-6 months).

The question

"What happens when I type www.amazon.com into a web browser and hit enter?"

Non-technical users are abstracted away from all of the systems and technologies that power an ordinary page request on the Internet. Although it may seem simple and straightforward, a lot of connected gears have to work properly for you to have a seamless browsing experience. If you perform a simple search on "technical product manager interview questions" on Google, you'll easily discover a variation of this question surfacing over and over again.

Why is this question such a popular one? It is because it tests the systems-level knowledge of the product manager, and provides a platform for the PM to put their technical know-how on display without explicitly coding on a whiteboard or referencing specific functions of programming languages. When this question is posed to a PM, there are three tiers of responses that are common among interviewees.

Expert-level knowledge: References DNS (including methods of load balancing and limitations), caching, CDNs, ARP, sockets, web stack, page rendering, load balancers, performance expectations, availability, SYN/ACK, TCP/IP, HTTP(S), user agent, security implications, and so on.

Basic knowledge: References DNS, CDNs, caching, TCP/IP, HTTPS, and so on.

© Aswin Pranam 2018
A. Pranam, *Product Management Essentials*, https://doi.org/10.1007/978-1-4842-3303-0_5

Lack of understanding: References DNS only, talks about how it hits a server, or fails to deliver an answer due to lack of technical knowledge.

In this section, we'll float between expert-level and basic concepts, boiling them down to understandable terms. The goal isn't to remember the details, but to burn the concepts deep in your mind so you can have a broad strokes view into how it all happens in the blink of an eye.

Let's get started.

Step 1: `www.amazon.com` is typed into the web browser

Self-explanatory. Fire up Chrome, Firefox, Safari, or Edge browser and type in the URL (in this case, amazon.com). Hit enter, and activate the set of digital dominos that follow.

Fun fact: Sometimes you will see references to `www.amazon.com`, sometimes to just amazon.com. The abbreviation www is a reference to the mostly deprecated phrase "World Wide Web" which gained prominence in the late 1990s. Today, in most cases, you do not need to use www in an address when going to a website, but some websites do still require it.

Step 2: DNS (Domain Name Server / System)

In its simplest form, the Internet is just a connected set of computers or servers that contain files that people want to access. When you input amazon.com in the browser, you're requesting a set of resources from a server that exists in the digital ether, and asking it to execute a particular task. In order to send the request to the right server, the Internet uses IP addresses to communicate. An IP address is a unique sequence of numbers used to identify devices connected to the Internet. In the case of amazon.com, we can find the IP address that corresponds to the website by using the "ping" command.

If you are on a Mac, use Spotlight search to open the Terminal app. Type in the command "ping amazon.com" and press enter to execute it. You should see the following screen returned:

```
●  ●  ○  ○              ⌂ aswinpranam — ping amazon.com — 80×24

Last login: Sun Jul 30 21:17:46 on console
[Aswins-MacBook-Air:~ aswinpranam$ ping amazon.com
PING amazon.com (54.239.26.128): 56 data bytes
64 bytes from 54.239.26.128: icmp_seq=0 ttl=231 time=82.430 ms
64 bytes from 54.239.26.128: icmp_seq=1 ttl=231 time=81.354 ms
64 bytes from 54.239.26.128: icmp_seq=2 ttl=231 time=81.309 ms
64 bytes from 54.239.26.128: icmp_seq=3 ttl=231 time=82.469 ms
64 bytes from 54.239.26.128: icmp_seq=4 ttl=231 time=82.317 ms
64 bytes from 54.239.26.128: icmp_seq=5 ttl=231 time=82.013 ms
64 bytes from 54.239.26.128: icmp_seq=6 ttl=231 time=81.258 ms
64 bytes from 54.239.26.128: icmp_seq=7 ttl=231 time=80.800 ms
64 bytes from 54.239.26.128: icmp_seq=8 ttl=231 time=93.176 ms
64 bytes from 54.239.26.128: icmp_seq=9 ttl=231 time=86.859 ms
64 bytes from 54.239.26.128: icmp_seq=10 ttl=231 time=256.522 ms
64 bytes from 54.239.26.128: icmp_seq=11 ttl=231 time=182.833 ms
64 bytes from 54.239.26.128: icmp_seq=12 ttl=231 time=112.448 ms
64 bytes from 54.239.26.128: icmp_seq=13 ttl=231 time=81.138 ms
64 bytes from 54.239.26.128: icmp_seq=14 ttl=231 time=80.370 ms
64 bytes from 54.239.26.128: icmp_seq=15 ttl=231 time=81.692 ms
64 bytes from 54.239.26.128: icmp_seq=16 ttl=231 time=110.773 ms
64 bytes from 54.239.26.128: icmp_seq=17 ttl=231 time=88.591 ms
64 bytes from 54.239.26.128: icmp_seq=18 ttl=231 time=82.451 ms
64 bytes from 54.239.26.128: icmp_seq=19 ttl=231 time=80.419 ms
64 bytes from 54.239.26.128: icmp_seq=20 ttl=231 time=81.077 ms
```

Ignore the rows and rows of data that show up, and focus entirely on the highlighted IP address (in this case, 54.239.26.128). This is the identifier for the server that our request to load amazon.com goes to.

Now, as a user, if we had to remember the IP addresses of every website we wanted to visit, we'd have to keep a paper Rolodex or Word doc handy. This also limits our ability to visit a lot of sites because the process becomes too cumbersome. Not ideal.

DNS (Domain Name System) solves this problem. Instead of remembering 54.239.26.128 each time we want to buy an item from Amazon, we only have to remember "amazon.com". DNS is a virtual phonebook; the URL is an easy-to-remember domain name that we're able to commit to memory, and DNS converts it into an IP addresses that finds the correct resource on the internet. Think about it like storing contacts on your phone; you can't remember the phone numbers of every contact on your phone, but you don't need to because they're saved behind a contact name.

To further illustrate how this system works, it's entirely acceptable to use the IP address in the search bar and get the same result.

Here, the IP address 54.239.26.128 is typed into the search bar.

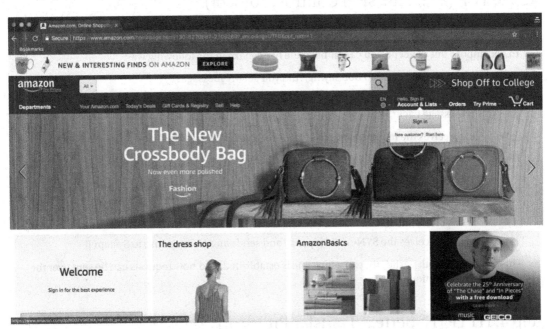

DNS finds the correct web resource, and the browser reverses the IP address to amazon.com for readability.

Now that we understand how DNS is used, it's important to keep in mind that web requests take time. Even if it's in the order of milliseconds, it can affect the experience of content delivery. To speed up the request each time, your browser will store data locally (known as caching). In the case of DNS, once we've accessed amazon.com once, there's no reason to hit the DNS each time because that slows performance. Instead, the browser will create a local DNS cache of the websites you've been to so the next time you visit amazon.com, it can directly you immediately to the website without hitting the DNS upstream. There are other caches (OS cache, router cache) along the way that can improve performance, but we'll leave them out since that's dipping too deep.

DNS isn't just one big server that all computers know how to reach. It is a decentralized system of servers that are provided by Internet Service Providers (ISPs) and network operators as resources to computers on their network. In addition, large companies like Google provide their own DNS services internally and to the public.

To further simplify, DNS follows the path defined below:

Browser cache (if website was accessed at least once) ➤ intermediary DNS ➤ root / authoritative DNS

The intermediary DNS is usually controlled by your ISP (Internet Service Provider) and configured automatically unless you change it, but the authoritative DNS is the source of truth that contains ALL of the webpages that are newly created. If you register www.newwebsite.com, it will be added to the root DNS and flow downstream to all of the domain name systems across the Internet. This is partly why you need to wait anywhere between 1 hour to 24 hours after buying a domain name to actually see your website up and running.

Fun fact: groups of websites have gone down in the past because hacker groups have targeted DNS specifically. If you disable the phonebook that controls Internet routing, people no longer can access the website in the way they're used to. However, if you know the corresponding IP address, you can access the website directly and circumvent the problem of failed DNS requests.

Step 3: TCP (Transmission Control Protocol)

TCP is an underlying protocol that powers communication of data between interconnected systems. In our use case, TCP establishes a line of contact with the server using a **handshake**.

To decompose this concept, you can think of the handshake in the following way:

- Alice sends a message to Bob saying, "did you get my message?"

- Bob sends a message back to Alice saying "Yes I got your message. Did you receive this message back?"

- Alice receives the message and says "Yes, I received your message back"

The technical implementation follows a similar exchange:

- System A (browser) send a SYN packet (small unit of data) to System B (Amazon server)

- System B receives the SYN packet, and sends a SYN-ACK response to System A

- System A receives the SYN-ACK response and sends an ACK response to System B

This confirms to both parties that an active line is established, and now requests can be sent over the established TCP connection.

Step 4: HTTP (Hypertext Transfer Protocol)

HTTP is an application-layer protocol that sits on top of TCP to enable web activity and navigation on the Internet. After the TCP connection is established, the web browser sends an HTTP GET request. A GET request basically says, "I want to GET some data from your server"; in our case, the Amazon landing page. The GET requests sends additional data in the header of the request called the **user-agent**, which communicates the user's browser and device type, in order to deliver the content in the relevant format, among other things.

Optional Step 5: Load balancing

A website at the scale of Amazon is hammered by millions of requests and transactions each day. If they only had one server to handle all requests, the site would go down immediately. To combat this situation, Amazon will have multiple servers across strategic geographic locations that can handle user requests. To decide which server to send your particular request to, they use a technique known as **load balancing**.

A load balancer (either hardware or software based) accepts a request, and uses a set of procedures to determine which server to forward the request to. In a simple case, let's say we receive 10 requests in the span of 1 second. A round robin method can be used to send request #1 to server 1, request #2 to server 2, request #3 to server 3, and request #4 back to server 1. This process continues in a predictable, repeatable manner so requests are evenly distributed. When it comes to setting up and using a load balancer, it is advisable to use two for the purposes of redundancy. If only one load balancer exists, and it fails for any reason, it can create a bottleneck that swallows up all the requests and prevents them from being routed to the web servers correctly. Using two load balancers that communicate with each other using a **heartbeat** (simple ping to see if the other is alive / active) protects the system and creates a fail-safe mechanism.

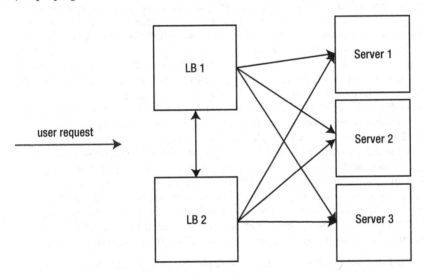

Optional Step 6: CDNs (Content Delivery Network)

A CDN is a system of distributed servers that organizations can use to deliver content to users in a faster way. For example, if a new startup wants to increase performance without buying expensive bare metal servers or spinning up virtual machines, they can tap into the power of a CDN and host their files on this widespread network of servers. Since CDNs are designed to have servers available in locations that deliver content to users quickly, the CDN servers will absorb the traffic and alleviate pressure on the startup's central hosting solution. Not all products or companies will need to use a CDN, but it's important to know they exist if scaling is called into the conversation. One popular CDN is Cloudflare.

Step 7: Web server response

The HTTP request sent earlier by the browser is accepted by the web server, and HTML content is sent back to the client browser. When the HTTP request is accepted, there is a web server (Apache, Nginx) that is responsible for handling the request, and a back-end programming language or framework (PHP, Ruby, Python) that handles what actions to take.

Step 8: Browser generates content

The server sends the requested content to the user's browser, and the HTML content is loaded, along with linked style sheets, scripts, and associated content. All of this comes together to display the www.amazon.com landing page.

Voila, we've covered the highlights of how content is delivered on the Internet! It's certainly possible to expand on each step, but this level of granularity is acceptable for a product manager's body of knowledge. Going a tier deeper in understanding is not expected, and is usually better left for a software engineering or technical architect interview setting.

Software Engineering: Through the lens

I am a software engineer who works with product managers on a daily basis. Week-to-week, product managers do a ton of research on where the market is headed, and based on their research, they come up with a product vision for the next generation of products. Additionally, they consult software engineers to see how much their product vision can become a reality. Product managers provide a lot of value because they are thinking about what is best for the customers. Their vision helps gain customer attraction to the product, and indirectly, they help drive the revenue for the company.

While it is not needed for product managers to have technical knowledge, it really helps the engineering team if they do. One of the primary reasons for this is because having the technical knowledge helps the product manager connect well with the engineering team, and have a clear end-to-end discussion of how a product might get built up. Additionally, while building a product, if there are technical obstacles, then a product manager's technical background really helps drive the product vision and decision forward.

I do have a couple of tips for PMs to work well with engineering teams. First, keep dreaming high. By dreaming high, a PM's vision really helps the engineer push for the best product out there. Second, when there is a problem, try to understand the problem and help the engineers come up with a better solution. Often times, without understanding the full picture, PMs often try to give an alternate solution which confuses the software engineer even more. So, it is really advisable to get a deeper understanding of the problem they are facing. Finally, while it is good come up with tight deadlines, realize that software engineers are humans too. A PM who treats fellow engineers as humans really stands out as way more likeable and efficient than someone who treats them as a working machine to fulfill their vision.

> – Ayanjyoti Ghosh, SDE at Amazon. Previously Software Engineer at Microsoft & Intel.

The web stack

Now that we have an understanding of the process of servicing a web request, let's cover the web stack. A **stack** is a collection of technologies that power a software product. A product manager will frequently be in the room for discussions regarding the stack, but they're not expected to contribute in meaningful ways that define the architecture. Still, it's useful to know the basic terminology so the entire conversation doesn't go over your head. Over time, as you close knowledge gaps, you can establish goodwill with the engineering team and make recommendations on frameworks, tradeoffs, and pros / cons of the design of the product.

In web programming, the two most commonly used stacks are **LAMP** and **MEAN**.

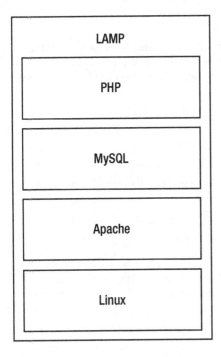

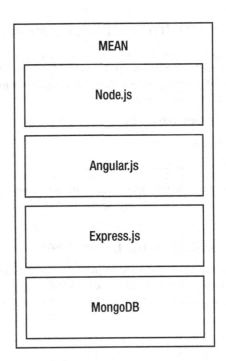

LAMP stands for Linux, Apache, MySQL, and PHP. Linux is the underlying operating system, Apache is the HTTP web server, MySQL is the database, and PHP is the back-end programming language. The MEAN stack stands for MongoDB, Express.js, Angular.js, and Node.js. In this model, MongoDB is the database, Express.js (known as Express) is a web application framework, Angular.js (known as Angular) is a front-end framework, and Node.js (known as Node) is a server-side framework. The LAMP stack was the popular choice in the last 5-10 years of web development, but MEAN is quickly picking up steam. It is becoming the preferred stack because the entire top-down stack consists of JavaScript as both the front and back-end programming language, whereas LAMP requires knowledge of JavaScript on the client end and a supporting back-end language like PHP. We won't be walking through each set of technologies listed, but it's worth looking into.

Front end vs. Back end

Up to this point, we've made several references to front-end and back-end technologies. Let's clarify the difference.

Front end: The software development that happens on the user-side. When you interact with buttons, forms, input boxes, images, banners and other elements of a webpage on a browser, all of this falls under the purview of the front-end developer. On this side, the primary technologies a front-end developer will work with are HTML, CSS, JavaScript, and any associated libraries (jQuery, Angular.js, etc.).

Back end: The code running on the back-end server that processes front-end queries and returns data back to the user. The back-end interactions are hidden from the user view, and relate to databases and application languages like PHP, Ruby (with the framework Ruby on Rails), Python (using the Django framework), and so on. The back-end language processes user logins, fetches your personalized content, manages state, etc.

Companies tend to hire front-end developers, back-end developers, and full-stack developers (engineers who can float between both disciplines) for web application development.

Getting started with front-end development

In this section, we'll walk through the basics of three languages that define front-end development: HTML, CSS, and JavaScript. Each language has a place and purpose, and come together to display a webpage and all of its elements on the browser you're using. If we simplify the job of each language down to two key terms each, they are all described in the following way:

- HTML - **content & structure**

- CSS - **styling & design**

- JavaScript - **action & interactivity**

As we step through each language, the distinctions will become clear and you'll naturally understand the separation.

HTML (Hypertext Markup Language)

HTML structures content using **tags**. A tag helps define an element on a page and render content on the browser. For an element to be considered valid, it must consist of an opening and closing tag with angle brackets, with the closing tag using a forward slash (/) to indicate closure.

Tag examples:

```
<div></div>
<p></p>
<title></title>
```

To visualize this, let's step through an example HTML file. Open up a text editor on your computer (Notepad++, Sublime Text, Visual Studio Code), create a file called index.html, copy & paste the following code, and save.

```
 ◀ ▶      index.html          ●
 1   <!DOCTYPE html>
 2   <html>
 3   <head>
 4   <title>random title</title>
 5   </head>
 6   <body>
 7
 8   <div>
 9   <h1>header1</h1>
10   <p>paragraph 1</p>
11   <p>paragraph 2</p>
12   </div>
13
14   </body>
15   </html>
16
```

- <!DOCTYPE html> - the DOCTYPE declaration indicates the HTML version of the file and doesn't require a closing tag. In this case, the version is HTML5 (default).

- <html> - the HTML tag is the parent element of every HTML file, and all elements fall between the start and end tags of this element.

- <head> - HEAD is used to capture metadata, non-visible content, links to stylesheets or scripts, and the title of the webpage.

- <title> - TITLE sets the browser tab title.

- <body> - The space for BODY is used for all of the content visible to the user and rendered on the browser.

- <div> - DIV is used to separate sets of data into logical groups. As you can imagine, a page with a lot of content can easily become difficult to manage, so you can use DIVs to create sections to reference later on.

- <h1> - H1 is the header tag, and bolds section titles and increases font size for headlines.

- <p> - The P tag (paragraph) is used to define a paragraph.

If we refer back to the index.html file we created and double click into it, a browser window will open and our page will be displayed.

header1

paragraph 1

paragraph 2

- The browser tab title is "random title", as defined by the <title> tag

- The header name is "header1", as defined by the <h1> tag

- "Paragraph 1" is defined by the <p1> tag

- "Paragraph 2" is defined by the <p2> tag

- <div> is hidden from the user view, and used only to the benefit of the developer to split content in the HTML file

In short, meshing tags together to display content is at the heart of what HTML does. To supplement your learning, go to popular web pages, right-click, and select "View Page Source". Since HTML is a frontend language, you'll be able to freely view how any website has managed to build out their frame (unless they purposely obfuscate the content).

Tags, tags, and more tags

<img> - Image tag

The image tag allows the developer to link images to the page. The <img> tag doesn't require a closing tag, but needs two attributes to be specified: src and alt. Src (source) points us to the location of the image so we can appropriately paste it into the page, and alt (alternate text) shows users a text explanation of the image if it doesn't load properly. Alt is also used for accessibility users who use screen readers to ingest web content, so it is important to include it.

Example image tag: <img src="aswin.png" alt ="profile photo">

<ul> / <ol> - Unordered and ordered list tags

To create list items in HTML, you can use the ordered list tag (<ul>) or unordered list tag (<ol>). The key difference is that <ul> will number the items in the list, whereas <ol> will be unordered. Both lists use the <li> tag to signify a single item in the list.

Example lists:

```
<ul>
        <li>Basketball</li>
        <li>Cooking</li>
        <li>Watching Movies</li>
</ul>

<ol>
        <li>Fishing</li>
        <li>Vegetables</li>
        <li>Snakes</li>
</ol>
```

<a> - Hyperlink tag

The <a> tag links one page to another (hyperlink). <a> requires the use of the "href" attribute to define the linked page, and the text in between the opening and closing <a> tag specifies the text you want hyperlinked.

Example hyperlink tag: <a href="www.linkedin.com/in/aswinpranam">Aswin's resume</a>

Nesting

Tags open up a world of possibility and flexibility to the developer, but often we'll want to combine individual tags together to take advantage of new functionality. For example, what if we want to create an ordered list of our favorite websites, with each list item hyperlinked to the respective webpage? That's where nesting comes in.

We're able to nest as many tags as we want, and it helps us structure our content in new ways. Just remember: we still need to abide by HTML rules and close each tag (if required) and be careful to close the tags in an inside-out manner.

Nesting #1: Linking an image to a webpage

<a href="www.linkedin.com/in/aswinpranam"><img src="aswin.png" alt ="profile photo"></a>

Nesting #2: Creating an ordered list of links

```
<ol>
        <li><a href="www.amazon.com">Amazon homepage</a> </li>
        <li><a href="www.google.com">Google homepage</a></li>
        <li><a href="www.facebook.com">Facebook homepage</a></li>
</ol>
```

Now that we've gone through the fundamental makeup of an HTML page and the basic tags that create the content hierarchy, let's put all of this together to build a personal profile page. See if you can understand the code, and how it corresponds to the finished output below.

Source code:

```
1   <!DOCTYPE html>
2   <html>
3   <head>
4   <title>Aswin's Website</title>
5   </head>
6   <body>
7
8   <h1>Aswin Pranam's personal page</h1>
9   <p>Welcome to my page! Please feel free to explore and reach out if you have questions.</p>
10
11  <img src="https://media.licdn.com/mpr/mpr/shrinknp_400_400/
    AAEAAQAAAAAAAAxAAAAAJGFlOTA5MWQ1LTQ4ODMtNDE3OS04ZmRhLTQ1YjNjNmFjMzgyYw.jpg" alt="profile photo" height="
    200px" width="200px">
12
13  <h2>Likes</h2>
14  <ul>
15  <li>Basketball</li>
16  <li>Cooking</li>
17  <li>Watching Movies</li>
18  </ul>
19
20  <h2>Dislikes</h2>
21  <ul>
22  <li>Fishing</li>
23  <li>Vegetables</li>
24  <li>Snakes</li>
25  </ul>
26
27  <p>If you'd like to get in contact, visit my LinkedIn profile <a href="http://www.linkedin.com/in/
    aswinpranam">here</a></p>
28
29  </body>
30  </html>
31
```

Profile webpage:

Aswin Pranam's personal page

Welcome to my page! Please feel free to explore and reach out if you have questions.

Likes

- Basketball
- Cooking
- Watching Movies

Dislikes

- Fishing
- Vegetables
- Snakes

If you'd like to get in contact, visit my LinkedIn profile here

And that's it! Next up, CSS.

CSS (Cascading Style Sheets)

CSS is used for styling, decorating, and presenting the overall aesthetic of the webpage. The profile page we created using HTML is a start, but it's barebones: no colors, font styling, or patterning. CSS works by using selectors to select elements on the page, then assigns a set of properties to those elements.

Let's look at a quick example. To begin, create a new file using your editor called style.css. Next, open index.html and add a <link> tag to the <head> section. The <link> tag connects CSS code to the HTML file.

```
1  <!DOCTYPE html>
2  <html>
3  <head>
4  <title>Aswin's Website</title>
5  <link rel="stylesheet" type="text/css" href="style.css">
6  </head>
7  <body>
8
```

Once the style.css file is linked, we can start altering the elements in the index.html file. To select elements to style, we use the HTML tag name. If we want to change the color of <h1> elements to red and set a background color of black, we can use the code below in style.css. In parallel, we can change all of the <p> elements to have a blue background color and a dotted border by using similar syntax.

```
1  h1 {
2      color: red;
3      background-color: black;
4  }
5
6  p {
7      background-color: blue;
8      border-style: dotted;
9  }
10
```

HTML + CSS profile website:

Likes

- Basketball
- Cooking
- Watching Movies

Dislikes

- Fishing
- Vegetables
- Snakes

It's not pretty, but it drives the concept home. The process of building a beautiful web page is painstaking, and a solid reason why we should thank our front-end developers and web designers.

One additional point to know about CSS is the concept of an ID and Class. In the above example, we chose to style headers and paragraphs, but the commands we coded styles every single header and paragraph on the page. What if we only want to target one header, or select paragraphs?

To do this, we need to open our index.html file, and add an ID or Class to the element we want to change exclusively. In our case, we can append an id attribute to <h1> and call it "aswin".

```
1   <!DOCTYPE html>
2   <html>
3   <head>
4   <title>Aswin's Website</title>
5   <link rel="stylesheet" type="text/css" href="style.css">
6   </head>
7   <body>
8
9   <h1 id="aswin">Aswin Pranam's personal page</h1>
10  <p>Welcome to my page! Please feel free to explore and reach out if you have questions.</p>
11
```

Then, we can replace h1 in the CSS file to #aswin and the styling that follows will only apply to the element with the ID.

```
1   #aswin {
2       color: red;
3       background-color: black;
4   }
5
6   p {
7       background-color: blue;
8       border-style: dotted;
9   }
10
```

IDs are defined using the "id" attribute, whereas classes are defined using "class" in the HTML file. IDs can only be used on one element, but classes can be assigned to multiple elements simultaneously for batched styling.

Content & structure: check.

Styling & design: check.

JavaScript

JS (JavaScript) is the third and most expansive language on the front-end web stack. JavaScript can be used for front-end interactivity, but it can also be run on the server as a back-end language using Node.js, or even as a desktop development language using third-party frameworks and libraries. If there's ever a time to master one language and one language alone, JavaScript would be a prime candidate for the top spot.

The purpose of JavaScript on the front-end is to enable actions across the website; button click responses, submitting content to the server, animations, and pushing / pulling content as needed. It's impossible to cover all the intricacies of JavaScript as a language in a handful of pages (refer to additional resources below for further learning), but I'll add a block of code with basic functions below for the curious.

```
1    // Variables (var) are named containers that store data. They must be declared, and can be used
2    // in the program instead of referencing raw values.
3
4    var monkey;
5    var bankaccount = 1000;
6    var car;
7    var sisters = 3;
8    var examplevariable = "Jeff";
9    examplevariable = "Rick"; // if you want to change a variable, all you have to do is define a new value
10
11   // Selection of elements can be achieved using document.querySelector, followed by the tag name.
12   // Once selected, you can manipulate the data in the tag and perform actions on the HTML file directly.
13
14   var header = document.querySelector('h2');
15
16
17   // Conditional branching describes the method of using if / else statements to split the end scenario
18   // into two or more buckets based on a true or false condition.
19   // For example, we can use if / else to return only men's clothing if the selected style is Male.
20
21   var shoesize = '9';
22   if (shoesize === '9') {
23     alert('We have shoes in stock!');
24   } else {
25     alert('Sorry, we are sold out!');
26   }
27
28   // To learn more, check out Javascript documentation and references online.
29
30
```

Additional Resources

- HTML / CSS

    • HTML & CSS, design and build web sites by Jon Duckett

    • W3Schools online web tutorials / documentation

    • Head First HTML with CSS by Elisabeth Freeman and Eric Freeman

- JavaScript

    • Javascript: the definitive guide by David Flanagan

    • Beginning Node.js by Basarat Syed

    • Pro Angular by Adam Freeman

    • Pro Mean Stack Development by Elad Elrom

- Back-end software development

    • Head First Rails by Thomas Asbridge

    • Django by Example by Antonio Mele

    • Murach's PHP & mySQL by Joel Murach and Ray Harris

    • Udacity / Coursera free online classes on back-end programming languages

Final Thoughts

Technical expertise can be a powerful differentiator for a product manager. Although not required, a high-level understanding of how a collection of technologies come together and the benefits & limitations of each is never a bad skill to possess. You're not an expert on web development after covering this chapter; not even close. But, breaking complex ideas down to simple terms hopefully has inspired you to learn on your own time. A lot of the technologies you interact with frequently can be mastered in a short time window, and it doesn't have to be just an engineer's task to think through decisions about architecture and technical design.

CHAPTER 6

■ ■ ■

SQL Quickstart

Now that you (hopefully) have a rudimentary understanding of the Internet and web technologies that power it, let's move forward to a skill that every PM needs in their toolset: SQL. SQL (pronounced "see-quill" or "S-Q-L" depending on preference) stands for Structured Query Language, and is used for creating, transforming, and manipulating data in a relational database. A relational database is an information system that exists to structure data in rows and columns for easy read and write alterations. For example, let's take a look at an example SQL database table for vehicle data:

ID	Make	Model	Color
1	BMW	328i	White
2	Mercedes-Benz	CLA 250	Black
3	Acura	TSX	Blue
4	Porsche	911	Red

As you can see, each column of data is indicated with a header label, and all fields are represented in rows underneath. If you're familiar with cells in Excel, the concept of how and why a table is structured in this way will become immediately clear as we walk through this chapter. At a basic level, SQL enables a developer or analyst to build new databases and tables in a quick, repeatable manner and add data to them easily. On the flip side, SQL can allow you as a product manager to pull data directly from the database without chewing up engineering cycles. PMs who can master the art of querying tables can save their development team significant time on data pull requests, and enable themselves to chop the data up in creative ways to identify patterns at will. Whenever an application requires back-and-forth interaction with a set of data (e.g., posts on Facebook, movie titles on IMDb, movies on Netflix, etc.), you can almost guarantee that a database is involved in some form or fashion. Although different implementations of relational databases exist on the market (MySQL, Microsoft SQL Server, PostgreSQL, etc.), the underlying syntax is common (if not identical) between all the products. We'll be using mostly mySQL syntax in this chapter since it is one of the most popular and widely used offerings on the market. In this section, we'll cover basic SQL statements used for data handling, walk through the process of joining sets of data together, and touch on advanced topics in a broad strokes view. Don't worry, it's easier than it sounds.

And with that, let's jump right into writing SQL statements!

■ **Definition** A "query" is a statement issued to a database to return information. In the scope of a SQL database, a query encompasses anything typed into a terminal or GUI (graphical user interface) that is a direct command for data retrieval.

© Aswin Pranam 2018
A. Pranam, *Product Management Essentials*, https://doi.org/10.1007/978-1-4842-3303-0_6

CREATE, DELETE, and SHOW database

Before we set out on a journey to harness the power of raw data and become SQL wizards, we need to create a database to store the information. A database is simply a collection of tables, and houses data for future use. For example, a car dealership database (car_db) can contain tables such as inventory_table (tracking available cars), orders_table (records all historical purchases), HR_table (employee information), and so on. As you'll soon notice as you step through this chapter, SQL is an intuitive language because it uses simple terms to define the commands. In this scenario, the statement to create a new database is CREATE DATABASE, and the action to delete the newly created database is DROP DATABASE. The same structure can be used to add and delete tables inside the databases as well (CREATE TABLE [name] & DROP TABLE [name]). Once the database is created and defined, we can populate it with tables and send commands for data retrieval.

Query:

```
1  //Create a database. Then, drop(delete) it
2
3  CREATE DATABASE example_db
4
5  DROP DATABASE example_db
```

To confirm that a database has indeed been created, you can use the SHOW DATABASES command. If a list emerges with the previously named database, then everything is working as intended. If a blank list is thrown back, then you may have to revisit your creation step.

Query:

```
1  //Show all of the databases that exist
2
3  SHOW DATABASES
```

SELECT statements

A SELECT statement is the most common SQL command used to retrieve data: it tells the database what data you want fetched. If we wanted to write a query that will return all of the data in our vehicle table (named example_table), we would issue the following.

Query:

```
1  //Selecting all of the data from
   example_table
2
3  SELECT *
4  FROM example_table
```

Result:

ID	Make	Model	Color
1	BMW	328i	White
2	Mercedes-Benz	CLA 250	Black
3	Acura	TSX	Blue
4	Porsche	911	Red

Let's break this command down.

1. The two forward slashes (//) denotes a comment to explain the query. It reinforces the goal of the query that we're executing, and only exists to help you, the reader, understand what we're doing. Also, ignore the line numbers. I'm using Sublime Text as my IDE (integrated development environment), and it automatically numbers the lines on the fly. They have no relation to the query being issued.

2. The SELECT defines the main command we want the database to interpret.

3. The asterisk (*) is a catch-all for everything in that table. It essentially translates to EVERYTHING in simple terms.

4. The FROM describes which table we want to pull data from (in this case, example_table).

5. Formally issue the command, and all of the rows and columns are displayed.

Great! But what if you want to return only the make and model of the car? Let's change up the original statement to fit our new requirements.

Query:

```
1  //Selecting only the make and model
   columns from example_table
2
3  SELECT make, model
4  FROM example_table
```

Result:

Make	Model
BMW	328i
Mercedes-Benz	CLA 250
Acura	TSX
Porsche	911

In this case, we're asking the database to return ONLY the make and model columns instead of the entire table. If the user wants to include the "color" column, all they have to do is add in "color" to the SELECT query after "model".

Simple so far, right? Let's keep pushing forward.

SELECT statements with conditions

At this stage, you may be wondering: "What about the rows? How do we prevent the entire data dump from being surfaced every time we run the command?"

Good question. Cutting and filtering the data in a useful fashion requires operating on both dimensions, so we use the WHERE operator to specify the constraints.

Query:

```
1  //Selecting only the result with an ID
   value of 1
2
3  SELECT *
4  FROM example_table WHERE ID = 1
```

Result:

ID	Make	Model	Color
1	BMW	328i	White

In addition to specifying values that already exist in the table, the WHERE operator can also be used for comparisons and logic operations (<, >, =, LIKE, and NOT). Imagine a table listing cost and locale of food items in a region, as shown below, and you were a PM tasked with completing a competitor analysis.

Item Number	Name	Price	Zip Code
132452123	Sunflower Seeds	$3.45	96035
43656455	Apple Pies	$12.44	39503
59049304	Nutella	$5.44	85033

If we were to kick off an assessment and wished to trim the data based on price and zip code, we could couple the WHERE operator with the AND operator to chain commands together, as shown in the following sample query.

Query:

```
1  //Select and return item number and name
   of products over $5 in zip code 85033
2
3  SELECT item number, name
4  FROM example_table WHERE price > 5.00 AND
   zip code = 85033
```

Result:

Item Number	Name
59049304	Nutella

SQL operator breakdown

AND: Both statements must be true for data to be returned.

```
SELECT *
FROM NFL_teams
WHERE name = 'Tom Brady' AND team = 'New England Patriots'
```

OR: Either the first condition or the second condition must be true for the data to be returned.

```
SELECT *
FROM product_info
WHERE price > 20 OR discount_status = 'clearance'
```

NOT: All data is returned except for condition specified by NOT. NOT is exclusionary, and exists to return the opposite of the specified state.

```
SELECT *
FROM universities
WHERE name IS NOT IN ('Cornell', 'Harvard')
```

The commands we've been issuing are on miniscule data sets with less than five rows, but using the WHERE clause coupled with complex operator combinations on tables with hundreds of thousands of rows (possibly millions) can lead to insights that influence product decisions and break the holistic data view into digestible chunks.

UPDATE table with new data

So far, we've been exercising our ability to read data from a database, but for data freshness and overall practicality, we need the power to update and add data. Using UPDATE, we can identify a row, set a new value, and finalize the change. Our example_table with vehicle data incorrectly uses a discontinued model name for Acura, so let's use UPDATE to correct this mistake.

Query:

```
1  //Update Acura model type from TSX to NSX
   for row ID 3
2
3  UPDATE example_table
4  SET Model = 'NSX'
5  WHERE ID = 3;
```

Table contents after UPDATE is run:

ID	Make	Model	Color
1	BMW	328i	White
2	Mercedes-Benz	CLA 250	Black
3	Acura	NSX	Blue
4	Porsche	911	Red

DELETE table rows

Conversely, instead of updating data from the table, the DELETE command removes rows completely. DELETE can be used with conditions, or as a blanket command using the structure DELETE [tablename] to clear all of the contents of a table, so be sure to exercise caution to avoid erasing all of your data with a mistake query!

Query:

```
1  //Delete the line item for BMW from the
   table
2
3  DELETE FROM example_table
4  WHERE Make = 'BMW'
```

Result:

ID	Make	Model	Color
2	Mercedes-Benz	CLA 250	Black
3	Acura	NSX	Blue
4	Porsche	911	Red

ORDER BY

The ORDER BY command is positioned well to sort data and trim the rows returned to a manageable size. ORDER BY takes column names as a parameter, and arranges them in ascending order by default, with an option to convert to descending by appending DESC to the end of the query. If the table you're dealing with contains thousands of rows and you want a subsection of the full view from a top down perspective, use the LIMIT command to restrict the number of rows that are returned.

Query:

```
1  //Order by MAKE and limit results to
   first two rows
2
3  SELECT *
4  FROM example_table
5  ORDER BY Make LIMIT 2
```

Result:

ID	Make	Model	Color
3	Acura	NSX	Blue
2	Mercedez-Benz	CLA 250	Black

JOINS

The last command we'll cover is the concept of a table join in SQL. Joins allow data from multiple tables to be combined using similar columns that exist in both tables. In total, four common joins are typically used to merge table contents together.

Left Join: all rows from the left table are retrieved, along with matching rows from the right table.

Right Join: all rows from the right table are retrieved, along with matching rows from the left table.

Innner Join: only matching rows belonging to both tables are retrieved.

Outer Join: retrieves all rows from both tables.

To better illustrate this point, we'll walk through each join type step-by-step using the following example tables.

Table 1. *example_table1*

ID	First Name
1	Grant
2	Rob
3	Femi

Table 2. *example_table2*

ID	Last Name
1	Tall
2	Lee
4	Haque
5	Oje

LEFT JOIN (also called LEFT OUTER JOIN)

A left join will return all values in the left table (the table defined first in the query) and join against all of the matching values on the right table (table listed after the LEFT JOIN indicator). Companies don't hold all of their data and information in one single database. Instead, grasping the concept of table joins will help you identify common fields and stitch the data together across tables. Aside from using the JOIN operator, we also need to use ON to establish which column we want to use to join the data. Both tables must have one column with a linking key for a join to be successful. A primary key is a distinct ID (e.g. integer) used to assign each row in a table a unique identifier. The foreign key is the mapping value; in essence, it is the same value that sits in another table that can be used to join the two together. The primary / foreign key paradigm can be hard to understand at first, so I recommend follow up research if the queries below are difficult to digest.

Query:

```
1  //Retrieve every row from the left table,
   and only matching rows from the right
   table.
2
3  SELECT *
4  FROM example_table1
5  LEFT JOIN example_table2 ON
   example_table1.ID = example_table2.ID
```

Result:

ID	First Name	Last Name
1	Grant	Tall
2	Rob	Lee
3	Femi	null

■ **Note**   the "null" value that surfaces when we return this set of data indicates no value in the right table that matches the ID of 3.

RIGHT JOIN (also called RIGHT OUTER JOIN)

A right join will return all values in the right table (the trailing table in the JOIN command) and join against all of the matching values on the left table. Notice that the positioning of the tables in the query doesn't change, since first placement signifies left table and second placement is associated with the right table.

Query:

```
1  //Retrieve every row from the right
   table, and only matching rows from the
   left table.
2
3  SELECT *
4  FROM example_table1
5  RIGHT JOIN example_table2 ON
   example_table1.ID = example_table2.ID
```

Result:

ID	First Name	Last Name
1	Grant	Tall
2	Rob	Lee
4	null	Haque
5	null	Oje

INNER JOIN

An inner join will return only the values that match in BOTH tables. Depending on what you specify as the join criteria, the results returned can vary between queries.

Query:

```
1  //Retrieve only intersecting rows (
   matching rows) from both tables
2
3  SELECT *
4  FROM example_table1
5  INNER JOIN example_table2 ON
   example_table1.ID = example_table2.ID
```

Result:

ID	First Name	Last Name
1	Grant	Tall
2	Rob	Lee

OUTER JOIN (also called FULL OUTER JOIN)

An outer join will return every row in both tables, even non-matching pairs. If the rows happen to match, then they will only populate one row. For example, in the resulting table below, we don't have one unique row for ID 1, Grant and another unique row for ID 1, Tall. Common records are merged together, and mismatched rows use the null designation.

Query:

```
1  //Retrieve every row from both tables (
   even non-matching)
2
3  SELECT *
4  FROM example_table1
5  FULL OUTER JOIN example_table2 ON
   example_table1.ID = example_table2.ID
```

Result:

ID	First Name	Last Name
1	Grant	Tall
2	Rob	Lee
3	Femi	null
4	null	Haque
5	null	Oje

■ **Note**   MySQL doesn't support FULL OUTER JOIN at the time of this publication. To replicate this function, you will need to use the UNION operator instead and thread together a left and right join.

Advanced topics

We've covered a lot in this chapter, but there's still a lot more to know about SQL and relational databases. If you're ready and willing to go deeper down this rabbit hole, I've brushed over some advanced topics below. Note that I've left out details and simplified a few of the concepts listed, but you will sharpen your understanding as you do more independent research. The goal is to get you curious enough to learn on your own and move closer to mastery at your own pace.

Indexing: Dealing with massive tables with millions of rows can be difficult from a data processing standpoint because the queries will take minutes (or even hours) depending on complexity and available processing power. To speed up the data fetch, you can create indexes against your database, and avoid having to rerun the entire query each time. To frame this in a simpler fashion, think about searching for a word in the dictionary. You can spend time flipping through the pages, one by one, until you finally arrive on the correct definition, or you can skip to the index in the back of the book and find the exact page without having to perform a manual search operation each time. A database table index allows you to do the same, and save processing time by avoiding unnecessary database operations.

Normalization: Falling in the domain of database design, normalization splits the data into logical tables so redundant work can be avoided. For example, imagine a 1,000,000 row table with name, address, and magazine subscription name. If John Doe has 12 entries in the table because he's moved a bunch of times, then we'll need to update his address in 12 different places the next time he moves (one time per row). Instead of this long and arduous process, we can split the main table into two tables: one for name and magazine subscription name, one for address and link the two with a set of primary and foreign keys. This way, if John's address needs to be changed, it only has to be updated in the address table one time.

Sharding: An advanced technique that splits the database into smaller chunks called "shards" to push across distributed servers. Sharding improves processing performance and enables segmentation of data based on permissions rules the developer creates (e.g., US users vs. EU users). At a local level, instead of running queries on your individual laptop or desktop, you can shard the data and process information across clusters in the cloud for faster results.

NoSQL: A new wave of databases that break free of the traditional relational model. noSQL databases are often used for big data sets, and can offer advantages over relational databases depending on use case.

ACID: Atomicity, Consistency, Isolation, and Durability. ACID comes into play when dealing with concurrent transactions in databases (checking out items, paying for goods/services) and guarantees the security, validity, and quality of the data in the event of an error or failure when transactions are executed.

Data sanitization / database security: Changes are made to a database based on the SQL queries that are issued to it, so we must be careful about protecting the back end from any malicious queries. Allowing a user to input data into an application that doesn't go through a proper sanitization process could leave your data vulnerable. A variety of front-end (input validation) and back-end techniques (query monitoring) can be leveraged to prevent SQL injection from damaging your products or applications.

UML: Unified Modeling Lanuage (UML) is a standardized method to visualize all of the design components of a system. UML diagrams are used to create schemas that map the tables to one another and describe the relationships between each entity (one to one, one to many, etc.). Before any development work is done, a well-crafted UML diagram can be a quick look into whether the system makes sense and data is appropriately bucketed into the right locations.

Informative…but why is this useful to me as a PM?

Whether you're joining a newly launched startup or a mature technical firm, both value two key variables: time and money. When you're engaged in an arms race of innovation against other companies, time is everything, and distracting engineering resources away from building hard features can be costly. A PM who can be a data wrangler and build their own view of the data without a helping hand can be a welcome relief to the engineers, and it can be a quick and easy way to get respect within the team. SQL is a language that can be learned in a short period of time at an intermediate level, so dedicating the effort to practice the commands and dig into the advanced topics will only be advantageous for you in the long run, and a data-driven PM is only made more effective with SQL expertise.

■ **Note**   Practicing with or running SQL queries should generally be done in a non-production environment. Running queries in a production environment risks exposure of sensitive information as well as affecting mission-critical operations. Generally, there is no good reason why you would need to query a production database rather than a copied version of that data on a completely separate non-production system. Following best practices ensures that you aren't the person making the news for deleting all of your company's data, or for having your laptop filled with sensitive data stored on it stolen from your car (encrypted or not).

■ ■ ■

CHAPTER 7

Industry Spotlight: Q&A with Vivek Bhupatiraju

Vivek is a Product Manager at TUNE, a mobile analytics and performance marketing platform. Prior to TUNE, Vivek spent time in technology roles at Accenture, Limeade, and Nordstrom. He holds a Master of Science in Computer Science from Georgia Tech and a Bachelor of Science in Informatics from the University of Washington.

What does the term product manager mean to you?

A product manager is above all an advocate for the user. Their primary responsibility is to ship the right product and get it in the hands of the intended user base. Find a problem, design a solution, and find a way to translate that into a product that's easy, effective, and complete.

Can you break down a "day-in-the-life" of a TUNE PM?

6:00 AM - Wake up. Listen to music on my Alexa. Get ready and head to work.

7:00 AM - On the bus. Listen to a podcast or read tech blogs.

7:30 AM - Look at industry related news, trends, competitor launches.

8:00 AM - Arrive at work. Reply to emails and slack messages.

8:30 AM - Make my to-do list for the day.

9:00 AM - Daily standup with engineering team.

9:15 AM - Product team weekly sync. Talk about what we did this week, hope to do next week, ask each other questions.

10:00 AM - 5:00PM - Depends on the phase of the project(s) but can involve:

Hopping on the phone with some customers.

Strategic thinking days.

Writing product specs.

Writing stories and backlog prioritization.

Wireframing mockups with the design team.

Whiteboarding technical architecture for a project with an engineer.

Data analysis using SQL, Spark, and Google Analytics to understand user behavior and measuring KPIs.

6:00PM - Bus home. Another email reply session.

7:00PM - Gym time or play basketball.

8:00PM - Dinner.

9:00PM - Read a book or spend some time writing.

What interested you initially about product management?

I enjoy looking for new opportunities, convincing the company that we should head towards this direction, and creating the strategy that will get us there. I realized that I would never truly be happy being a developer or designer, and needed a role that will allow me to dabble evenly across all areas. Achieving balance can be difficult, but that's where I thrive.

How do you deal with failure as a PM?

I tend to look at failure analytically by measuring the impact of the failure and thinking through the decisions that lead to that product failure. Where did we go wrong? What was the inflection point (if any)? Failure is not the end of the world because you now have a set of lessons to draw from. Even data can be misleading if read improperly, so gut decisions can often lead to better outcomes in circumstances where you feel you have an incomplete picture.

What emerging technologies excite you most for the next five years?

Artificial intelligence / machine learning and virtual / augmented reality. ML will allow us to drive better insights and create new job opportunities that don't currently exist. With AR / VR, we can develop new experiences that existed only in our imagination previously.

How do you avoid burnout and keep a healthy balance between work and personal life?

Multitasking can often lead to burnout, so I try to fall back into solving one problem at a time. Juggling too much on your plate can leave you feeling like you're not inching towards a solution, and can be detrimental in the long run, which leads to half baked products. Prioritize, set realistic goals, and recognize that healthy living and exercise are critical in keeping the brain sharp.

What tools make your life easier as a PM?

- Trello for personal task management

- Jira for project management

- Balsamiq for rapid wireframing

- Evernote for note taking

- Google Docs for specs

- Google Forms, SurveyMonkey for customer surveys

- GA, SQL, Spark for analytics

- Intercom for customer messaging and go-to-market

- ProdPad for roadmap strategy and feature request management

What advice do you have for readers who want to get into product but have no prior experience?

I was in this situation, spending time as a technical program manager before transitioning into a product role within my organization. The best advice is to try to do some product work at your current company with spare cycles. I set up bi-weekly 1:1s with 3-4 PMs to learn more about their job, and asked them if there was something I could take off their plate. A couple of them let me write some specs which they peer reviewed, and also let me drive the product until final shipment. I ended up working more than the typical 40-hour week at first, but eventually the company recognized I had a knack for it and promoted a full-time change. Being in a supportive enterprise that allows you to grow and develop your talents in parallel areas makes the task of transitioning much simpler.

CHAPTER 8

■ ■ ■

Analytics are everything

"There are two possible outcomes: if the result confirms the hypothesis, then you've made a measurement. If the result is contrary to the hypothesis, then you've made a discovery."

—Enrico Fermi

In the information age we're currently occupying, data is king. Machine learning-enabled startups and products are being touted as the silver bullet to combat tough problems, and companies are investing heavily in data analysts and scientists. The hype around learning from patterns in data is at an all-time high, and organizations want to cash in on the gold rush as soon as possible.

Putting aside the mania surrounding big data, the longstanding principle of "if you can't measure it, you can't improve it" still applies to every software product that is user-facing. User actions, behaviors, and patterns of thinking can be captured using a variety of techniques, and the data can tell us things about the product at scale that aren't immediately obvious when testing with a limited user set.

In addition, the data we choose to collect and analyze gives us a set of targets to shoot for. A mobile application may track one-time downloads as the key metric, whereas an enterprise application could focus on subscription retention or churn as a guiding data point.

A product manager routinely needs to communicate progress and product success to an audience of stakeholders, and a combination of carefully selected metrics and data points can be the best way to describe the current state of affairs. Data analytics serves to provide insights, rank the user's flow of attention, and help PMs make better business decisions.

Analytics vs. Metrics

Before we start talking about the types of metrics to collect and the analytical tools to use, we need to define the two terms to solidify our understanding of the distinction.

- A **metric** is a unit of measurement that tracks one point of data.

- **Analytics** are the output of the process of transforming raw data (metrics) into actionable and strategic business insights. In other words, using the metrics you've collected to answer previously unanswered questions.

Analytics and metrics work hand-in-hand: first we come up with the right metrics to track, then zoom out and examine the relationships between the collected data.

© Aswin Pranam 2018
A. Pranam, *Product Management Essentials*, https://doi.org/10.1007/978-1-4842-3303-0_8

Selecting metrics for measurement

There is no "one magic metric" that every PM needs to flag for collection. Collect too little data, and you run the risk of missing patterns that lie below the tip of the iceberg. Collect too much data, and you could lose time parsing through all the information (especially if the repository is sizeable in nature). At a high level, we can hypothesize the general questions we want to answer through our metrics:

- Do users like the product?

- What causes users to stop using the product?

- How do users find out about the product?

- What features do users love? Hate?

- Are users able to navigate through our product with ease?

- What drives revenue in our product?

- What can be improved?

Once this is set, huddle with the team and management to think through the success criteria. Is it to maximize revenue? Grow the user base exponentially? Sunset (remove) features that aren't well performing or frequently used? Brainstorming will align goals, and you can form the metrics around the main product objectives. Metrics that guide key decision making are called **key performance indicators (KPIs).** Companies will tie KPIs to financial, business, and other success criteria, and setting a mix of realistic and stretch goals for the KPI goals keeps the team focused and efficient.

■ **Note**   Metrics can be deceptive. For example, imagine a small gaming startup preparing to launch a mobile app. A product manager may want to use "number of total downloads" as the target metric to maximize, but this can be misleading. A million users can download the app, but if you don't measure a complementary metric like weekly or monthly active users, you can miss out on stories the data is trying to tell. If a million users download but only 1,000 are consistently using the app every month, that can signal a major issue.

Types of metrics

Metrics indicate success or failure in whatever you're measuring, but without categorizing them properly, you could end up mixing one type of metric with another, leading to messy final insights and scrambled reports. To cover all of the bases when choosing trackable metrics, answer the following questions in the six categories as you put together a data analytics strategy: financial, business, product, process, people, and user. Use the categories and questions to frame the thinking when making the conscious decision on what to track versus what to ignore.

Financial Metrics

- How much money are we currently making?

- What are the revenue goals for the next year? Next 5-10 years?

- What are the biggest financial risks for our company? Industry?

- What is our annual growth rate?

Business Metrics

- What is our projected market share?

- How will we handle competitors?

- What partnerships can we strike with industry players?

- What acquisitions can we make?

Product Metrics

- What problem are we solving?

- Do people care about the product?

- Do they naturally recommend the product to their friends and colleagues?

- What features are unused?

- Does the product perform well?

Process Metrics

- Are we effectively following a framework or process for development?

- What are the primary concerns around our current processes?

- Do we document enough?

- Are we using the right software tools?

People Metrics

- Are people happy in the organization?

- Do employees feel satisfied by the work they're doing?

- What's the best way to reward high-performers and vice versa?

- How do we incentivize the team?

User Metrics

- Who is our target demographic?

- What will cause users to stop using our product?

- What will users pay for the product?

- How closely do we examine direct user feedback?

Metrics that matter

In the search to find the perfect mix of metrics to harvest, there are a baseline set of data points that need to be mentioned. Every product will not find the following list of metrics relevant, but in general, they'll come up over and over again in product discussions throughout a PM's career, and knowing the meaning behind the name and/or acronym is handy.

- Conversion rate
  - The number or percentage of users that complete a desirable action or goal (e.g., clicking on a banner ad or subscribing to a monthly service).

- Bounce rate

  - The percentage of users who leave the website or app after the first page or opening interaction.

- Churn rate

  - The percentage of users who leave or stop using a product or service within a specific timeframe. Also referred to as the attrition rate.

- Growth rate

  - The percentage increase of a unit of measure (users, revenue, etc.) over a period of time.

- Customer lifetime value (CLV)

  - The amount of revenue expected from a single user through the lifetime of their engagement with the product or service.

- Monthly recurring revenue (MRR)

  - Measurable and predictable revenue per month calculated by multiplying number of users with amount paid per month.

- Daily / Monthly active users (DAUs / MAUs)

  - Number of unique users who actively engage with the product or service on a daily or monthly basis.

- Average revenue per user (ARPU)

  - Total revenue divided by the number of total users.

- Customer acquisition cost (CAC)

  - The cost of acquiring a customer (marketing and promotions) divided by the number of customers acquired during a period of time.

- Customer satisfaction (CSAT)

  - A percentage or numerical representation of the user's level of happiness or satisfaction with customer service interactions.

A/B Testing

A/B testing (also known as split testing) is an effective method to measure performance of two websites by comparing one version (A) to another (B). Often used to measure conversion and engagement, A/B testing is extremely helpful in finding out which variation of a particular page resonates most with the end user. To set up an A/B test, use a tool (Optimizely, Google Analytics) to inject a snippet of Javascript code, then create two distinct webpage versions, and run the different pages on live users. If you notice an uptick in one experiment versus another, you can swap out the old page with the new and continue tweaking the elements on the page to maximize conversion.

In Figure 8-1, the first Apple.com webpage (A) uses the "Say hello to the future" header.

Figure 8-1. *Apple Website (Version A)*

In Figure 8-2, the second webpage (B) uses "the future is crystal clear" as the header. In this A/B test, Apple can surface both pages to a statistically representative sample of users, and record the header that results in more iPhone X sales.

Figure 8-2. *Apple Website (Version B)*

Multivariate testing

For products and companies with an established user base, A/B testing may only scratch the surface since only two variants of the webpage can be tested at one time. With multivariate testing, we can test as many possible permutations of the website as we want, granted we have the user base to split the pages amongst.

In multivariate testing, the original page is split into smaller components. In the page shown in Figure 8-3, we can mark the top navigation bar, the title / header, and hero image all as disparate components to use for our multivariate experiment. Now, let's say we want to test the following areas by:

- Changing the product ordering in the navigation bar (2 variants)
- Changing the iPhone X title / header (3 variants)
- Changing the hero image (2 variants)

Figure 8-3. *Apple Website (Multivariate Test)*

With the components identified, we can tell that there are 12 possible combinations possible ($2 \times 3 \times 2 = 12$). From this point on, we can use industry tools to push out 12 versions of the page to end users and track conversion and other related metrics.

Analytics: Through the lens

To me, analytics have always been an unlock of stories that otherwise would be untold. Often, analytics provide the sole answer for issues that drive reduced efficiencies, non-optimal processes, or fractional revenue and margin potential for organizations. In today's landscape, where companies are rigged with antiquated technologies and solutions, I continue to see analytics unveiling significant opportunities, with projects, programs, and investments all rallying around the narrative that they identify.

In a similar vein, yet independent in value, metrics and KPIs create the ability to quantify achievement and impact in unparalleled ways. In their truest form, the beauty is that they can't be gamed. You either hit them or you don't; you reap the rewards or incur the penalty. Other communicated factors for success are softer; manipulated and massaged messages telling the story that you'd like or the one others would hope you to believe. While these messages are cloudy and limit transparency, well defined metrics can become your single points of truth and KPIs can help to raise your accountability both internally and externally.

To consistently deliver value and authentic results, designs of metrics should always be distilled down to data which materially impacts the process at hand while striving to avoid unnecessary information. Metrics benchmark your success, and infer what improvements can be made in future sprints. In my opinion however, KPIs are more pronounced, and at their best signify strategic objectives and goals leading to your overall success. Given the growth of both small and large technology integrators it has become imperative for me to ensure that KPIs (often contractually), orient teams to a single mission. Unfortunately, there have been times this wasn't the case, and we have felt the pain of spin and discord. However, when designed correctly, and supported by tactical metrics, the results have helped ensure successful delivery of many of our initiatives. In looking forward, my hope for the generation of technologists on the horizon is that they leverage the power and influence of analytics, metrics, and KPIs and use them to quantify their value and impact to their organizations.

Grant Small, Nike Supply Chain Technology Consultant

Drilling Deep with Google Analytics

Google Analytics is a robust analytics engine developed to help websites maximize advertising return on investment (ROI) and track detailed behavioral metrics. The tool itself is easy to use; just set up an account, copy a few lines of Javascript code to inject into your own product, and the results will autopopulate in the dashboard once user interaction begins.

In Figure 8-4, the Google Analytics demo instance is up and running, giving us a peek into the main dashboard view. A grouping of high-level metrics is shown (Users, Revenue, Conversion rate, Sessions) along with sections to go deeper in the left-hand navigation pane.

Figure 8-4. The Google Analytics demo

Google Analytics splits the reports into four sections: Audience, Acquisition, Behavior, and Conversions. Since the tool collects so much information at once, the subsections are helpful when honing in on related slices of the analytical data set.

For a product manager, the behavior flow is a critical view to develop familiarity with (Figure 8-5). It tracks the number of users who touch the landing page, and shows a raw user count for each set of possible interactions that users could follow in the product. This report can identify areas with high rates of exit, and confirm if the product is intuitive enough to guide users from start to finish without hand-holding.

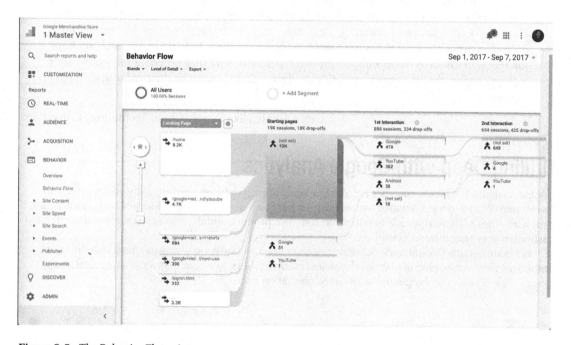

Figure 8-5. *The Behavior Flow view*

Another helpful view to keep an eye on is the funnel visualization (Figure 8-6). The funnel begins with a top-level action or function (in this case, the shopping cart) and tracks a user's journey through the flow to show how many end up past billing & shipping, payment, and finally to checkout. The funnel can expose bottlenecks in the system as users are closing in on the main goal, and elements that prevent them from a successful positive exit scenario.

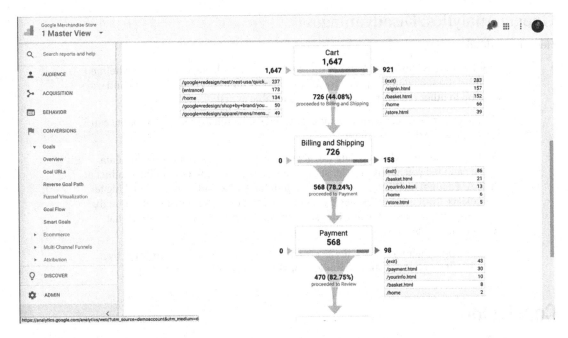

Figure 8-6. *The funnel visualization*

Experiment with the Google Analytics dashboard and make a note of the sections of data that suit a particular product's industry, type, technology stack, and use case. Then, create a set of reports that return only the set of numbers you need to make informed decisions. Everything else can be treated as random noise.

Google Analytics: Advantages

Here are the advantages of Google Analytics:

- Powerful: loads of functions and reporting capabilities integrated into the platform.

- Easy setup: simply inserting a snippet of code gets the tool up and running.

- Free (for basic tier): no cost to low-traffic products and/or services.

- Cross-platform: records analytics on web, mobile, and other devices.

- Customizable: flexibility of the tool allows for the product manager to create product-specific reports and data captures.

- Documentation & training: the community for GA is vast, and tons of tutorials exist for learning the ins-and-outs of the platform.

- Common across the industry: almost all companies in advertising, ecommerce, and marketing use Google Analytics (or are aware of the tool). Knowing and understanding the platform is a transferrable skill no matter where your career takes you.

Google Analytics: Disadvantages

Here are the disadvantages:

- Information overload: the first few times you use the tool, you may be overwhelmed by all of the segmented reports. Focus first on only high-level metrics, then find ways to loop in other reports that were unapproachable at first.

- Steep learning curve: slicing and dicing the data to be relevant to your product can be a difficult task for first-timers.

- Tells you what, not who: the data will give you aggregate numbers and blind data, but it can't tell you about the user specifically. Is the user who bought the product at 5:00 AM a night owl? Is the customer who purchased the ball gown also looking for a necklace from other websites? If your engineering team is sophisticated enough, building out your own tracking infrastructure can start to answer questions that Google Analytics can't.

- Cost: stepping across the free tier to enterprise can increase the monthly bill by a significant amount ($4,000), so budget considerations will come into play.

Conclusion

Collect everything you can, then trim it down. The biggest mistake you can make is to assume you only need X amount of data points, then realize later down the road that X + Y is what you REALLY needed. Even if you have to find the needle in the haystack later on by storing so much data, it's worth it compared to making up for lost time and starting the collection today as opposed to yesterday.

Collect, track, measure, and influence. You will be at a grave disadvantage if you don't.

CHAPTER 9

■ ■ ■

Software Development Methodologies

"But I should caution that if you seek to plot out all your moves before you make them—if you put your faith in slow, deliberative planning in the hopes it will spare you failure down the line—well, you're deluding yourself. For one thing, it's easier to plan derivative work— things that copy or repeat something already out there. So, if your primary goal is to have a fully worked out, set-in-stone plan, you are only upping your chances of being unoriginal."

—Ed Catmull

Software engineering is messy; products can break in a production environment, engineers and designers can roll off a project at any given moment, and pressures from upper management can intimidate teams into cobbling together disjointed pieces of functionality for the sake of hitting project milestones. Traditionally, software development was thought of as a predictable process. The product owner would gather requirements, provide a rough estimate of each step in the stream of work, and more or less guarantee a firm delivery date. This process, known as waterfall, held innate advantages that made directors and managers happy, but it often resulted in a subpar final product.

Realizing the straight-line manufacturing process of developing products wouldn't translate well into the software domain, the agile manifesto was born. The credo, created by a group of technologists and forward thinkers, described a brave new world of developing technology in the following way:

> **"We are uncovering better ways of developing software by doing it and helping others do it.**
>
> **Through this work we have come to value:**
>
> **Individuals and interactions over processes and tools**
>
> **Working software over comprehensive documentation**
>
> **Customer collaboration over contract negotiation**
>
> **Responding to change over following a plan**
>
> **That is, while there is value in the items on the right, we value the items on the left more."**

And thus, agile development practices were brought to the forefront. In this chapter, we'll cover waterfall and its shortcomings (along with a brief set of advantages it possesses). Then, we'll take a peek into the new agile standard, and the most popular framework implementation known as Scrum.

© Aswin Pranam 2018
A. Pranam, *Product Management Essentials*, https://doi.org/10.1007/978-1-4842-3303-0_9

What is waterfall?

Waterfall, named after the top to bottom flow found in nature's waterfall, is a sequence of steps that lead to a predictable outcome. The model is commonly found and used in the fields of manufacturing and construction, but early days of software development adopted waterfall as the logical way to build tech products. In Figure 9-1, you can see how it begins with the top-level step of requirements definition, and falls down the waterfall until we hit deployment and maintenance. Each step is completed independently, and the next stage cannot begin without successful completion of the one that precedes it.

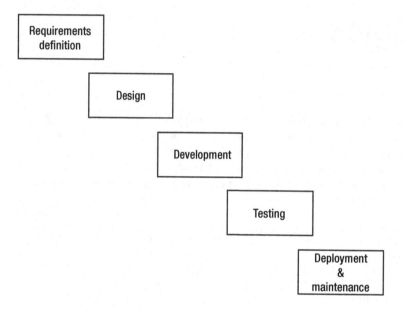

Figure 9-1. *The Waterfall model*

Advantages of waterfall

- Deadline-driven: team agreement on timeframes for delivery and exact delivery date. Each block is assigned a time estimate, and the deployment finish line is fixed.

- Strict: project teams are held accountable for their development tranche and held to a specific set of expectations.

- Documentation: the straightforward nature lends itself well to team members producing documentation religiously for each step.

- Design is locked down early: product design is formalized early and management knows exactly what they're getting upon completion.

Disadvantages of waterfall

- Estimation is generally incorrect: requirements will change (especially on external client projects), and waterfall can't accommodate for mid-project shifts well.

- Inflexible: product development is rigid and allergic to change of any kind once the development phase is entered.

- Non-iterative: chain of steps is one-way; no room to revert back to a previous step for cyclic improvement.

- Expensive rework: technical and design changes involve adding time to the end of the project and extending the deadline beyond what was initially predicted.

Agile

Agile, an umbrella term used to categorize the collection of frameworks aimed at improving upon the waterfall method, is the antidote to the headaches and disadvantages in the order of activities previously described. To provide an easy-to-understand comparison between waterfall versus agile, let's think about a structure we're all familiar with: a bridge.

Procedurally, the waterfall method to building a bridge lacks ambiguity and has a set of goals that mirror historical projects. Bridges have been built for centuries, and all of the possible failure scenarios can be predicted beforehand with thorough analysis and keen attention to detail. A base foundation is laid down, a scaffolding is erected to support the weight of the structure, and a combination of wood, concrete, or steel is introduced to drive the project to a finished state. Construction lends itself well to waterfall because, in 95 percent of cases, we're not creating anything novel. Institutional knowledge can be leveraged and combined with external factors (weather, location, etc.) to produce a predictable end result.

With agile, the process is quite different.

Instead of building the structure entirely off a set of initial requirements, we start by tying the two endpoints of the bridge together with a piece of string (Figure 9-2). Why? Because we don't know how to build what we're building yet. Software development is relatively new each time, and we need a trial-and-error approach to understand the right way to put the pieces together. Tying the metaphorical string together gives us an MVP, and leaves room to test assumptions. Once the string is tied, we present the design to management and/or customers and source their feedback. If they're happy with the way it looks, we allow the team to proceed with development.

Figure 9-2. *Tying the endpoints together*

After the first approved run, we connect both endpoints with just one straight line of bricks (Figure 9-3). Again, not a heavy lift in terms of development, but each micro-step inches us closer to the finished project. Once again, we demo the incremental improvement to management and/or customers, but this time, they're unhappy. They initially thought brick was the material to use, but they push back and inform us that steel with gold plating satisfies the requirement better. For the project team, this is valuable information.

If we had begun the project with the assumption that the bridge will be entirely made from brick, the presentation at the end of all the hard work would have fallen flat. Back to the drawing board.

Figure 9-3. *Joining the endpoints*

To offer a parallel scenario related to software, let's say the project team decided to use XML to structure and transport data, but the client's existing systems use JSON for API requests. The early callout enables the team to adapt quickly, but the same ask at the end of the project would have been costly and time-consuming.

After multiple iterations of laying down just one line of gold-plated steel beams, the client is again satisfied. From this point, we lay down multiple beams and iterate. Each time a major component of the bridge is built, we demo for the client or end-user to get proper approval, then mobilize the team to start the next iterative cycle. Once all of the development phases are complete, we're left with a bridge that the client and project team are satisfied with (Figure 9-4). Software development is about moving fast and making things, and agile allows us to flex the framework in a way that creates an original, functional product. Out of all the frameworks available, we'll dive into Scrum at a deeper level and give you the tools to kickstart your own agile projects.

Figure 9-4. *The final bridge*

Scrum

Scrum, developed at the tail end of the twentieth century, aims to reduce defects, improve quality, and reduce the probability of project failure and dissatisfaction. It establishes a set of best practices for developing software, and is in use at Fortune 500 companies as well as established startups. In this section, we'll walk through all of stages of a Scrum process and deconstruct the vocabulary, roles, and outcomes. We'll also cover basic elements of the framework that you can start implementing as soon as possible into a product development cycle.

Structure

Scrum operates in a cyclical manner; instead of stages being independently set from start to finish, we find a framework that relies on a rinse and repeat model of product innovation. At the onset of Scrum, we develop a product backlog. This is a prioritized running list of every feature and requirement that the product will need to be considered "done." Once the master backlog is curated, we move items off of the backlog into a sprint backlog. A sprint is a two-week cycle of product development in which one modular piece of software is designed, built, and tested. The Scrum team will calculate what can reasonably be finished in a two-week timeframe, and estimate the level of effort for each feature. Then, the product manager will prioritize the estimates into actionable and realistic sprint workflows.

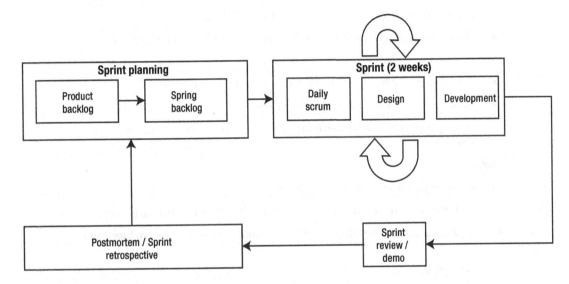

Figure 9-5. *The Scrum process*

Once the items are set in the sprint backlog, we officially kick off the sprint. During the sprint, we use a daily standup meeting each morning to track and record progress, and collaborate in unison with design and engineering teams until we've hit the requirements to satisfy the "definition of done". The definition of done is a set of acceptance criteria that acts as an indicator to the team that a requirement or feature is complete and ready for review. Once the two-week window expires, the chunk of completed work is moved into the sprint demo, in which the client or customer provides feedback and suggests changes for the features deployed. Finally, the team huddles for a retrospective to understand what went well, what can be improved, and prepare themselves for planning the next two-week cycle.

■ **Note**   Two weeks is the most commonly used time span for a sprint, but teams can extend to four weeks or shrink down to one week if necessary.

Roles / Artifacts

A Scrum team will typically have six to ten members responsible for driving the product to completion. A number smaller or larger than the six to ten window may experience issues with running a tight Scrum unless they have an experienced PM at the helm steering the ship.

The makeup of the team includes:

- A product manager

  - Responsible for running a successful Scrum

  - Prioritizes and builds product backlog

  - Communicates with client to define requirements / features

  - Provides a consistent vision and end goal throughout the development lifecycle

- Scrum master

  - Role often played by the PM, or TL (technical lead) in some cases

  - Removes roadblocks for the engineering team

  - Tracks progress burndown and ensures the team is on track to complete sprint items

- Scrum team

  - Mix of designers, developers, and supporting staff

  - Well-oiled group engaging with each other closely to deliver the final product

In addition to the team dynamics, Scrum requires the following artifacts to be produced and maintained:

- Product backlog

  - Master log of requirements (features to be built) that is routinely updated and revised. The PM is the owner of this artifact, and works closely with the team and customer to keep this up-to-date after each sprint.

- Burndown chart

  - A graphic visualization of the work completed in a sprint and the work still pending. It's a useful tool for the team to reference as they set sprint goals and navigate their way through development.

- Sprint backlog

  - Contains a subset of the product backlog that is committed by the team to complete in the sprint. The PM and team estimate the time required for tasks in the product backlog and moves them into the sprint backlog based on achievability. The sprint backlog is new at the start of each sprint, unless tasks were unable to be completed in the previous sprint and need to be transitioned over. Old sprint backlogs and burndown charts are documented to create a knowledge repository.

User Stories

As features are added to the backlog, they are re-written in a format known as a "user story." User stories are the preferred method for defining requirements because it uses lay terms to clearly communicate the feature to the wider Scrum team. In doing so, the story helps the group reach a common understanding of what has to be built to solve the problems users face. A user story generally adheres to the following structure:

As a [user type], I want to [insert requirement here] in order to [enter user goal here]

Let's take a look at sample user stories to drive the point home.

- As a user, I want to easily navigate through the application to quickly find the files I'm assigned to complete in order to complete my assigned tasks on time.

- As a doctor, I want to view patient data from anywhere in the world in order to assist my client base efficiently.

- As an administrator, I want to add and remove users to the platform in order to prevent unauthorized access.

- As a lawyer, I want to highlight legal documents in the mobile app to bookmark items for follow up later.

- As a power user, I want to assign hotkeys to simplify multiple-click tasks into one button press.

When defining requirements, we'll be faced with bodies of work that are too big to categorize as just one user story called **epics**. An example of an epic could be "As a user, I want to view a web dashboard after the results are submitted in order to manipulate the data." This particular piece of work is massive, and will need to be broken down into smaller stories that can fit within the scope of a sprint. The product manager's job is to logically cut and slice the user stories into a state where they can be implemented without slippage of timelines.

Scrum Meetings

Everyone hates meetings. They're bloated, and productivity proportionally decreases relative to the amount of people in the room (or virtual conference). In Scrum, the need to meet face-to-face is done in a focused and calculated way. Each meeting serves a purpose, and the potential to deviate away from the topic at hand is limited because the Scrum Master keeps everyone on track. In the scope of a well-run Scrum engagement, there are four essential meetings that everyone will be participating in.

Meeting Name: **Sprint planning meeting**

Duration: 4 hours for 2-week sprint, 8 hours for 4-week sprint

Purpose: The product manager will lead a session to move items from the product backlog to sprint backlog. A rough estimation of effort will be assigned to each item, and the entire 2-week sprint will be finalized. The development team will work with the PM to reasonably estimate how much can be accomplished, and everyone will commit to delivery once estimates are finalized.

Meeting Name: **Daily standup / Daily Scrum**

Duration: 15 minutes at the beginning of the day

Purpose: A status update sync that occurs at the top of each workday. Each team member will answer three questions: what did you do yesterday, what are you planning on doing today, and are there any blockers or impediments? Standups keep everyone aware of the development being done, and catches issues as they happen in real time.

Meeting Name: **Sprint review / demo**

Duration: Based on need (1–2 hours)

Purpose: Product is demoed to clients / customers to source feedback and receive clearance to continue onto the next sprint cycle. Demoes always show a live walkthrough of working features, as this is a key advantage of agile because the stakeholders can see the product being put together incrementally as the weeks go by.

Meeting Name: **Sprint retrospective / postmortem**

Duration: Based on need (1–4 hours)

Purpose: The retrospective serves to regroup the team after a sprint to discuss what went well, what could be improved, and what pitfalls can be avoided for the next sprint. The PM will also review the burndown chart and calibrate the velocity (measure of work a team completes in a sprint) more accurately for future cycles.

Work estimation

Before the product manager sits and thinks through the prioritization scheme for the product backlog, each item's level of effort needs to be estimated. Although Scrum doesn't prescribe any particular method for doing so, a few common approaches exist.

Planning poker

- Each member of the Scrum team receives a deck of cards with numbers ascending in value (1, 2, 3, 5, 7, 10...) or arranged in the Fibonacci sequence. The product manager will announce a requirement, answer any questions, and ask team members to place a card face down on the table estimating the effort required to complete the task. Once everyone has placed their cards, the estimates are revealed and discussed. Variance in the scores are discussed and discrepancies are settled. The PM will either accept a revised value that the team agrees upon or ask the team to retry the exercise to see if a natural convergence of values occur.

T-shirt sizing

- Similar to planning poker, except numbers are replaced with t-shirt sizes (XS, S, M, L, XL). This approach is effective for estimating relative work effort, but the drawback is a lack of granularity. For example, is a Large task double the effort of a Medium? Or only one incremental step above?

Bucketing

- The team starts off by using a whiteboard to draw a set of buckets (categories) to use for requirements grouping. Next, one item will be chosen at random and placed in one of the buckets based on team discussion. This will be the pivot. All of the team members will select a requirement, ask themselves if it is less or more work than the pivot, then place it in the corresponding bucket. This method is faster than planning poker, and encourages collaborating amongst team members. It can, however, drown out softer voices in the room since not every participant is required to provide their input in a free-for-all.

AGILE: THROUGH THE LENS

With Product Management of any kind, the primary responsibility is speaking to the customer and creating structure for engineering, all while owning revenue-modeled planning. PMs often encourage change in the development methodology, and promote better-faster-smarter-cheaper systems. Agile methodology makes their influence even stronger, allowing software to arrive faster with higher quality. That translates into improved revenue, higher predictability, and measurable savings in both cost and time.

While I was consulting with Accenture, the assigned client was one of the largest telecommunications companies in the country. Their objective was to roll out (from scratch!) an e-commerce and e-services platform so that customers can seamlessly purchase hardware and associated network plans. As Product Owner, my responsibility was to facilitate delivery. Working under the Agile model, we deployed monitored releases to subsets of customers to identify possible early features and track usability. Based on powerful customer feedback, the development team would consume prioritized user stories off a dynamic backlog, which was reviewed and updated to reflect internal conditions and external opportunities. Over numerous iterations, estimation and judgment of progress became better via cultivated KPIs, and we were able to rollout to larger and larger subsets of customers until the platform eventually went live.

In the context of releasing the most quality software in a timely and efficient manner, Agile methodology is a sure-shot winner. However, it also means there's a lot more on the Product Manager's plate, which is already filled with a wide range of ownerless and nebulous tasks. In my most successful work environments, Product Managers are often paired with 1-2 Business Analysts, thereby separating task management from decision making. As Agile models drive the need for more day-to-day involvement between PMs and development teams, it's important to ensure PMs aren't burnt-out in pursuit of a great burn-down chart.

Ariv Adiaman, Founder of Vozhi LLC. Previously Product Owner at Accenture, and Program Manager consultant at Microsoft

Advantages of Scrum

- Batched design and development: Design and development are conducted in unison, and rework of requirements or code is cheap. The batched nature of functional duties lends itself well to change, and this is key for fast-moving product teams.

- Working demo: Every sprint produces either a high-fidelity wireframe, prototype, or slice of working product to showcase for the client or customer. This continuous feedback loop is a tool for communicating progress to the stakeholders, and keeps both parties on the same page.

- Progress updates: Burndown chart tracks progress and enables the product manager to send weekly or bi-weekly updates out to relevant recipients.

- Iterative feedback loop: Feedback, feedback, feedback. Iterative development leaves no question unanswered and no feature untested from a user need standpoint.

- Daily standup: A quick, effective meeting at the start of the day keeps people informed on what is being done and identifies risks or slowdowns early.

- Improved quality: Every step is tested and verified, so the resulting product is high quality and battle tested by the end user.

Disadvantages of Scrum

- Scope creep: The dynamic nature of the product backlog makes it an easy target for stakeholders to add more and more requirements to the plate. It is up to the product manager to say no and avoid scope creep, which is extra growth and functionality beyond what was initially agreed upon.

- Commitment is key: Everyone needs to buy into the agile methodology and dedicate themselves to the process. If team members are doubtful of the direction, or distract themselves from the structure, it can easily throw the project off the rails.

- Cannot accommodate large teams: Coordinating the work items and responsibilities of teams in the high double digits is near impossible in Scrum (but doable under specific circumstances). Splitting the workgroup into smaller Scrum teams can be a way to mitigate this risk.

Do I need to religiously follow this framework?

Absolutely not. Engineering teams will conform to a style that meets the need of their organization and product type. In a large enterprise, Scrum is a refreshing way to speed up product development and deliver higher quality products, but a startup may find a stripped-down version of Scrum to be suitable for their scrappy, do-or-die culture. Introduce the agile mentality, and experiment with it until you've tweaked and fine tuned the technique.

Final Thoughts

To prepare yourself as a true agile practitioner, further study is encouraged. Exploring literature specifically dedicated to breaking down each layer of the process is useful, and going as far as becoming a Certified Scrum Master (CSM) can improve a project team's confidence in your ability to execute a framework correctly. Alternatively, other agile frameworks such as Kanban and Extreme Programming (XP) are also popular Agile methods, and exploring the pros and cons of each will put you in a position to make the right framework call for your own projects. As you progress through your own set of experiences with agile, a natural style will emerge organically. Some PMs will stick to Scrum principles very precisely, whereas others will develop a distinctive working style that works for them. There is no right or wrong way to be agile; iterate on the framework itself and the right path will reveal itself.

■ ■ ■

CHAPTER 10

Industry Spotlight: Q&A with Sean Ammirati

Sean helped found and successfully exit three companies after dropping out of graduate school. Today, he is a Partner at Birchmere Ventures, a seed stage fund with offices in Pittsburgh and San Francisco. He also is an adjunct professor of entrepreneurship at Carnegie Mellon University and recently authored The Science of Growth: How Facebook Beat Friendster--and How Nine Other Startups Left the Rest in the Dust. You can learn more about him at seanammirati.com

What does the term "product manager" mean to you?

To me, a product manager is really the "CEO" of a specific product. They are responsible for making tradeoffs and establishing the product vision and roadmap based a variety of inputs, including conversations with customers and each of his/her teams especially sales and engineering. In fact, in very early stages of a startup, the product manager hat is often worn by the CEO. Obviously, as the startup scales, it's important to create a product management function within the organization.

What is one thing that PMs can do immediately that will improve the way they build world-class products?

Go visit some customers and once you're done, go visit more. As I love to say to my students at Carnegie Mellon, 'the facts are outside the building'. It's so tempting to get trapped behind your email and attending those "critical" internal status meetings. However, world-class products are LOVED by their customers and it's so important to talk to them to make sure your product is getting that love.

As a venture capitalist, how do you gauge product vision when investing in seed-stage startups?

At the stage we invest, it tends to be very conversational. One question that I've found very helpful to ask is: "If your business succeeds, what does the world look like in 3–5 years?" I intentionally don't ask the question in a way to lead them to their financial projections (we'll get to that discussion much later). I want to know 'what the world looks like.' Great entrepreneurs create the world the way it ought to be. In general, the entrepreneur's passion comes through when answering the question, first about the broken things they are fixing, and then how that will deliver value to their customers and ultimately their startup.

© Aswin Pranam 2018
A. Pranam, *Product Management Essentials*, https://doi.org/10.1007/978-1-4842-3303-0_10

What present technology trend (VR, ML/AI, cryptocurrencies) are you bullish on for the next decade?

I'm excited about all three of those trends for the way all three will likely transform how we work, live and play over the next decade. However, given our focus and expertise as a fund, I am particularly excited about ML/AI's impact within enterprises. I recently wrote a letter to our LPs (the investors in our fund) about why I think this is such a big trend and how we are investing against it. I decided to publish it afterward. If you're interested, you can read it on my Medium page: `https://medium.com/@SeanAmmirati/`

What advice do you have for a nontechnical founder who wants to raise money and build a tech startup?

First and foremost, you need to recruit a technical co-founder. Keep in mind that technical leaders have a lot of options at this point. When you ask them to join you, they aren't going to simply build what you have in mind without any input or questions. You need to convince them of your vision and specifically that you've done the hard work of talking to customers to validate elements of that vision. If so and it excites them, then you can discuss them investing the most valuable asset they have (their time) into your startup. At that point, it makes much more sense to talk to investors about raising money as the team is such a key element of any early-stage investment thesis.

CHAPTER 11

■ ■ ■

Deconstructing System Design

"Design is not just what it looks like and feels like. Design is how it works."

—Steve Jobs

First, a product manager is a strategist. Aside from the day-to-day decisions being made that influence the current portfolio of products, your responsibility and expectation of forecasting into the future makes you a "technology prophet". Often, you'll be faced with problems that seem too big to solve. Once you get past the initial stage of panic, you'll refocus and think "there's no way this can be broken down to manageable chunks." Finally, as you exit the final phase of insecurity and doubt, you'll grab a cup of coffee, focus, and get to work.

In this chapter, I'll walk you through the components necessary to break down conceptual and system design problems, and go through two sample scenarios to frame the correct way of thinking. The design problem can take one of two forms: conceptual or technical. Conceptual system design problems train your brain to adopt a design thinking mindset, and technical design problems couple your technical skill set and critical thinking abilities to arrive at an optimal solution. Peeling back the layers, forming a view of what works or doesn't work, then retrying will play a recurring role in your career as a PM.

■ **Note** In technical roles, system design refers to questions that ask about topics that include:

Availability

Concurrency

Networking

Performance

Reliability

Software stack tradeoffs

Since deep technical expertise is not assumed for this book, we'll cover a general conceptual design question, with a bit of light exposure to the technical side just for breadth.

© Aswin Pranam 2018

A. Pranam, *Product Management Essentials*, https://doi.org/10.1007/978-1-4842-3303-0_11

Probing

If someone asked you the following question, how would you attack it?

"Design a toaster"

Some would start listing off a set of materials, metals, and labor expectations needed to build the toaster. Others would sit in silence; frozen and unable to find the words to express their confusion. A small minority would take a deep breath, remain calm, and begin the first step of probing. In the context of breaking down a conceptual problem, the single most important thing you can do is ask questions. Assumptions, especially those that you hold true based on your experiences and expectations, are dangerous.

You: "OK. So i'm assuming this is a standard, run-of-the-mill toaster?"

Random person: "Not exactly"

You: "Hmmm does it use different materials?"

Random person: "Irrelevant"

You: "Ummm is the end user unique for this product"

Random person: "Yes, this will be a toaster for blind users"

BINGO. Let's probe further, to see if there is anything else we're missing.

You: "Are there any other unique properties that set this toaster apart?"

Random person: "Yes, it runs entirely on solar power"

Impractical, but it gives us yet another data point to work off of. If a PM jumped right into solving the problem from the jump, not only would context have been lost, but the solution would be completely incorrect. Before anything happens or projects enter the planning stage, ASK QUESTIONS. Understand the entire problem space, and cover all areas of ambiguity. Assumptions will mislead you, so probe, probe, probe.

Identify pain points

After probing and coming to terms with what needs to be delivered, the next step is to identify pain points with the current product in the market (in this case, a toaster). It doesn't have to be comprehensive, but a quick and dirty list of problems you've encountered with the current standard is a sure-fire way of picking out pockets of opportunity.

Pain points (toaster)

- No loud audio feedback once toasting is complete

- Manually need to load items into the toaster

- Does not consistently toast products the same way (bread slices vs. bagels vs. waffles)

- Poor visual design; ugly

- Toaster has a temperature dial, but I, as the user, don't know what the ideal temp for items are

Glancing over the list, there may be additional points you'd include in your own list. Others may call out pain points that aren't necessarily true in the wild (e.g., industrial toasters have repeated beeps that alert the user of a job completed). The main takeaway is that everyone's list will differ because we don't have a landscape view of every feature combination of product "X" on the market, but we can move ahead and prioritize what we have regardless. In the scope of a well-functioning toaster, audio feedback is a low priority (except in this case, where we're dealing with blind users!). However, a feature that removes the temperature dial and replaces it with buttons or a touchscreen for bread, bagels, waffles, and other items could add more utility for the user.

Think about requirements

After pain points are considered, the stage is set for requirements collection. The final outcome needs to be an exhaustive list of mission-critical features all playing a distinct role in producing the best possible product in the end. For example, if this a toaster for blind users, using visual cues are not the optimal way to describe the state that the product is in, so we can explore other ways like the use of auditory feedback or tactile feedback through the use of braille characters, universal symbols, and so on. Create a list of everything that will contribute to the final design, and keep the user's needs at the top of mind when jotting them down. Just remember that a massive laundry list of every single feature or function is not the right way to go; this doesn't show creativity or strategic thinking. Instead, focus on the innovative new goals you anticipate the user accomplishing with your requirements baked into the final output.

Understand the market

After the requirements have been defined and finalized, the next step is to understand the market. At this stage of the game, you need to ask yourself questions along the following lines:

-   What is the total market size for this product?
-   How would I raise awareness of this product's existence?
-   How would I source feedback on the quality of this product and how well it satisfies user needs?
-   How would I price this product?
-   What are the metrics for success?

Quite often, back-of-the-envelope calculations can be made to size a market in a rough and dirty way based on limited information. Let's walk through a sample estimation question together.

■ **Question**   Estimate the size of the disposable diaper market

---

Assuming we're estimating for the United States market, we know that the total population is around ~300 million (closer to 320 million, but for estimation questions we don't need to be precise).

Next, the average life expectancy of a human being is around 75-80 years old, and assuming a balanced distribution, around 3.75 million people are included in each age group (300 million / 80 = 3.75)

Since children stop wearing diapers around the age of 2 and a half (reasonable guess), then we can say the total addressable market is 3.75 million (0-1 years old) + 3.75 million (1-2 years old) + 1.875 (2 - 2.5 years old) = 9.375 million

Out of the addressable population size of 9.375 million, let's estimate that 90 percent of the children in the group wear disposable diapers. We can assume the rest wear cloth diapers or use other methods of disposing waste. Note: the 90% is a rational guess based on my personal assumption. Saying 100 percent is unrealistic, because not every kid wears a diaper, but on the flip side, using a number like 40-50 percent is being too conservative (and probably wrong).

So, if we use the 90 percent figure, we can take 9.375 million and multiply it by .90 (90% in decimal form) to arrive at 8,437,500.

But we're not done yet. 8,437,500 assumes just one diaper for each kid for the year (which is obviously incorrect). Since we know a year has 365 days, and a child wears around five diapers a day (another reasonable estimate), we can say one child wears 1,825 diapers per year.

Multiply 8,437,500 (amount of kids who wear diapers per year) with 1,825 (amount of diapers one kid wears per year) and you get 15,398,437,500 or ~15.4 billion diapers per year.

At this point, you've applied critical thinking, broken a problem down to basic components and reassembled the pieces to a logical final number, and proven that you can deliver a step-by-step, structured approach to problem solving.

BUT, there are ways to go further down the rabbit hole and increase the level of confidence in the estimate:

- Adults wear diapers too. If we find a way to estimate the number of adults / seniors who wear disposable diapers, we can merge that number into the total and improve overall accuracy

- We assumed five diapers a day, but that number could be conservative. If you can think of a way to better justify five or change it entirely, it can influence the answer

- Our assumption was that the population is evenly distributed across each age group. Do you have information to prove or dispute this presumption?

- List goes on and on...

For back-of-the-envelope estimations, assumptions are critical; they're the only way you can move through the problem and navigate your way to a solution. You won't have to run back-of-the-envelope questions often, but the process of solving one is valuable regardless because you'll face real-life situations that require this form of intuition and structured approach.

Arrive at a solution

After considering the markets and end users of the product, you'll arrive at a final solution for the conceptual design.

To maximize the accuracy of your solution, keep the following in mind:

- Focus on clarity

  - There is no correct answer for an open-ended product design question; only your answer. Back it up using your own perspective, and stand by the decision you made. In real life, new product innovation will follow a similar process of research, design, and iteration, and flexible thinking is absolutely necessary to come up with a reasonable solution.

- Pressure test your solution

  - In a work environment, your product roadmap and vision will constantly be called into question and attacked. As the leader, it's your job to not only put the team at ease, but ensure them that you've thought through all of the areas of concern.

    –   Be creative

- In the toaster prompt, most people immediately think of toasters as they exist today, and marginally improve in one way or another. But what if you proposed an entirely new solution? The "job-to-be-done" is toasting pieces of bread, so why do we automatically assume the current technology satisfies this requirement in the most optimal way? Coming up with brand new, untested solutions can be refreshing, and provides evidence of creative thinking. Thousands of items from the past haven't been improved upon for centuries (check out Bill Gates' condom challenge), so reset your thinking and disregard the norms set beforehand.

And that's it. We haven't covered all aspects of conceptual product design (not even close), but we brushed over examples of things to consider and factors to keep at the top of mind. Integrate the product design mindset into your daily thinking, and it'll aid you when dealing with ambiguous, abstract problem scenarios. In the next section of this chapter, we'll walk through a common technical example in a compressed fashion. I don't expect you to understand every layer if you're not technical, but I'll simplify as much as I can and condense an hour-long answer into a couple pages. At the very least, it will give you insight into what a technical system design question looks like end-to-end.

Design a URL shortening service (bit.ly or TinyURL)

Background

A URL shortening service takes a long URL such as
www.exampleurl.com/kjsgklj34opi2rkm32dlm23doih232f4iotj34itp23i3jo25/?q=43k42lk3nfl23 nfin32i and converts it into something like www.short.ly/54jdn. With this application, a user will be able to navigate to a website (let's call it short.ly) and see a single input text bar and submit button. The user will then be able to enter a URL, hit enter, and the page will return a shortened URL.

Probing

A technical system will have layers upon layers of complexity. To begin, we'll want to pose questions to get a simplified picture of the features, constraints, and expectations of the system we're designing for.

    –   Can users name the shortened URLs?

    –   Do we need to establish a character or length limit for the URL?

    –   How long will shortened URLs remain active? Do they ever expire?

    –   Can users edit the long form URL associated with a shortened URL?

    –   Can short URLs be deleted?

    –   How much traffic do we expect per month for short.ly?

    –   Do we need to validate links before being submitted to the page?

    –   Should we test if a long link is active? If the link is broken, should we automatically wipe from our database?

    –   and on and on...

High-level design

Our shortl.ly web application will simply accept a short.ly URL (let's call it a short link) and redirect it to the user defined longer link (let's call it the target URL). Since we'll need to store the short link -> target URL association, we'll use a database to record the data. This relationship of A -> B mapping is referred to as a **key-value pair**.

Our simple "Links" table would therefore have a column for short link and another column for target URL. We'll want to include other points of information such as number of impressions/clicks, timestamp, and so on, but that's out of scope for this exercise.

Next, we'll need to generate a unique short link for each target URL that users enter into the application. To do this, we can use a **hash** function. A hash function can take a long URL and output a fixed-size unit of data.

Example:

www.exampleurl.com/klji34honweklnfaewiofhjrgk4j3kj3lj34

-> hash function -> **74h2nt**

www.exampleurl.com/klji34honweklnf

-> hash function -> **r87j3d**

www.exampleurl.com/klji34honweklnfk394hf237fh32

-> hash function -> **jd93nd**

The hash function demonstrated above takes a URL of any length, and always outputs a unique six-character value. Since the name of the game is URL shortening, a hash is perfect because the output in terms of length is predictable. Note: hundreds of hash functions exist, and you can dig into the math behind how hashes work if you desire. However, it's worth noting that **hash collisions** can occur. A hash collision happens when two inputs go through a hash function and result in the same hash. Let's assume that we don't have to worry about collisions for this case.

To bring it all together, the following set of steps will tie the experience together:

> user hits the short.ly landing page

> user types in "www.cnn.com/reallylongurl/unreasonablylong/shortenthisplease"

> user hits enter

> short.ly runs the "www.cnn.com/rea...." URL through a hash function

> the hash function outputs a 6-character hash: 5n3i6b

> the hash is stored as the key (first column) in our database, along with the long URL in the second column (value)

> short.ly website refreshes and shows the user the shortened link: short.ly/5n3i6b. Notice here that the hash is appended to the short.ly link after the forward slash.

> user navigates to short.ly/5n3i6b, which hits an API call that checks the associated target URL

> user is redirected to the target URL webpage

This is the bare minimum of expectation for a system design interview. More detail is required, along with a deep dive of the systems involved aside from just the database on the back-end. In addition to a 10,000-foot walkthrough, the following areas potentially need to be covered:

- Security

- Availability

- Performance

- Load balancing

- Costs

- Redundancy

- Caching

- Scalability

- Replication

- Networking

System design questions are difficult and extensive, but touching on them can be beneficial for a product manager. Reading a blog like www.highscalability.com on a recurring basis can help you pick up tidbits here and there that contribute to your technical arsenal, even if you only understand 10 percent of the content at first.

Additional Questions

For extra practice, take a look over the questions and design scenarios below. If the method of approach isn't immediately clear when it comes to arriving at the answer, start breaking them down into smaller components and ask yourself how you can reason up from there. In the paraphrased words of Elon Musk, boil everything down to just the basic principles, then put those mental Lego blocks together to get the final answer.

Back of the envelope:

- Estimate the number of laundromats in your city

- How many people wear hats in the summer in California?

- How many tons of pork are produced in the United States each year?

- How many mobile phones are recycled each year?

- Estimate the probability of finding a lost coin on the beach (nickel, dime, penny, or quarter)

Product / System Design:

- Design a theme park

- Design Facebook's news feed

- Design a concert hall

- Design Yelp

- Design a simple to-do list application

PART III

Design Foundations

CHAPTER 12

■ ■ ■

Mindful UX

"Most business models have focused on self interest instead of user experience."

— Tim Cook

Users, including yourself, are generally lazy and impatient. We don't like to wait for pages to load, hate long sign-up flows, and despise the idea of a shipping window that exceeds seven days. Our attention is currency, and companies are doing everything they can to keep us coming back to their products. Every point of frustration, every ounce of friction, and every moment that makes you say "I must be dumb...I can't figure this out" is all contributing to the user experience of the product you're interacting with.

To better explain the idea of user experience, let's walk through the process of attending a football game. Browse tickets, purchase a seat, then print on paper and bring to the venue. Once you get there, stand at the security gate, pick up concessions, and walk to your assigned seat. At each interaction point in this user journey, elements of the event chain can make or break the experience. Ticketing agency website running slow? Leave and go elsewhere. Only expensive seats left? Oh well. Security line taking forever? What a waste of time.

Now, let's say we introduce a new fastpass product specifically aimed at solving this problem. For a small premium, our service will assign you a personal concierge, handle ticketing and transportation to the venue, escort you to the front of the line, and have your concessions waiting for you at the ticketed seat. All merged into a seamless, easy experience.

Back to technology. Every human being has used a product that made them feel stupid, or annoyed them to no end. A TV remote. A government registration website. A gaming mobile app with unresponsive interaction points. User experience takes a human-focused view to solve these issues instead of pinning the blame on the user. When designing software, we need to think about how it will be used by us and others. In this chapter, we'll walk through principles of UX design, and understand UX research techniques you can immediately apply to strengthening your product experiences.

User Experience (UX) vs. User Interface (UI) design

Simply put, user experience is the ease of use and enjoyability of using a product, whereas user interface design is concerned with the look and aesthetics. For example, the simplicity of putting headphones in your ear that automatically connect to Bluetooth as soon as it senses your ear is UX, and a glossy, colorful body to an app or website falls in the realm of user interface design.

User experience is criminally underrated, partially because it is still misunderstood. A near perfect user interface doesn't automatically aid the user in reaching an end goal state without UX considerations that are baked into the design process. Factoring in time for UX research and paying close attention to end-user interactions can debunk assumptions made about whether a user does X or Y when they have your product in their hands.

© Aswin Pranam 2018
A. Pranam, *Product Management Essentials*, https://doi.org/10.1007/978-1-4842-3303-0_12

UX principles to live by

Consider the following five principles:

- Don't make the user think: A momentary pause, confused look, or a full stop in engaging with the product are clear signs that something is wrong. If users can't figure out how to use something within a couple seconds, then it's a product issue.

■ **Note** There's a terrific book called *Don't Make Me Think* focusing strictly on UX in web / mobile environments. I highly recommend checking it out.

- Trust established design patterns: Names and logos of products / services are left or center aligned at the top. A hamburger or three bar icon signals a settings drawer. A scroll bar indicates a high-low setting for a component. Years and years of product use has primed us to engrave certain types of imagery into our mental model. Don't reinvent the wheel and send the user on a wild goose chase for the areas they're familiar with or expecting in a complete product.

- Add moments that matter: Small UX Easter eggs delight the user and convert them into a walking billboard for your product. Take special care in crafting the experience and remember that user experience is a journey, not a destination. There is no "perfect experience". Improvement is ongoing.

- Hide away the details: The user doesn't care how the metaphorical sausage is made. Hide away technical details and keep the internal exposure of the product to a minimum, unless it enhances the experience.

- Keep it simple, stupid: Each additional screen or click is a potential dropoff point. The more inputs, the higher the likelihood of the user abandoning the flow.

Affordance

"...the term affordance refers to the perceived and actual properties of the thing, primarily those fundamental properties that determine just how the thing could possibly be used. [...] Affordances provide strong clues to the operations of things. Plates are for pushing. Knobs are for turning. Slots are for inserting things into. Balls are for throwing or bouncing. When affordances are taken advantage of, the user knows what to do just by looking: no picture, label, or instruction needed."

Don Norman

Blue underlined text sends an implicit signal that an element is clickable. A progress bar tracks a moving state for completion of a task. An envelope communicates a mail or inbox function. Our interactions with technology and software in the past have developed patterns in our mind that are intuitive and easy to follow. When designing products, keep track of consistent themes previously used and tap into them. Using help text is necessary when explaining complex actions, but proper visual affordance cues can clear up chatter on the digital canvas and present a cleaner look. Symbolism is a core part of UX, and affordance helps translate concepts and ideas from the physical space to software.

Additional examples

- Three upward curved lines to represent Wi-Fi
- Magnifying glass for "Search"
- A country flag for localization
- Grey out elements to indicate inactivity or disabled features
- Red text or icons for incorrect inputs or "Danger" signs

UX Research Techniques

Let's go through some useful research techniques.

Personas

A persona represents an average user of the soon-to-be developed product (see Figure 12-1). It can range from brand-obsessed individuals to elderly folk who have special considerations. Developing a diverse range of personas help understand the unique needs of each end user, and puts the team in a space to put themselves in lives of the people they don't have time to interact with. A persona can have as much or as little detail as the team needs, but the exercise is crucial to understanding motivations, behaviors, and concerns each profile will inherently have.

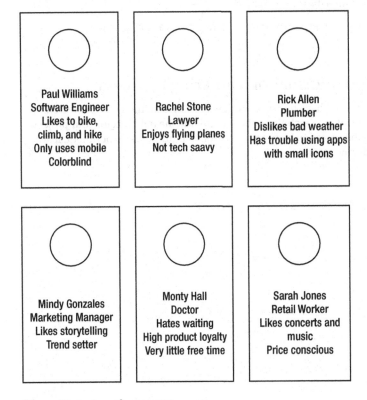

Figure 12-1. *Sample personas*

Diary study

To further inquire into the daily habits of your potential user base, pursuing a diary study can yield higher-fidelity results. A diary study involves recruiting a random, representative sample of key user personas, and asking them to record their day-to-day routine in blocks of time. At the conclusion of the study (or during regular checkpoints), the diaries are collected and examined to pool feedback into the product pipeline.

Surveys

If time is of the essence, and the PM requires a larger pool of participant responses, conducting surveys can be a worthwhile use of time and resources. Craft a set of open, clear questions and deploy to hundreds or thousands of people at a time. Using a service such as Amazon Mechanical Turk can widen the number of responses for pennies on the dollar.

Tips for developing targeted questions

- Decide whether to use open-ended questions (fill in the blank, paragraph responses) or multiple choice. The results will vary based on which method is agreed upon.

- Source email address or phone numbers for additional follow up (with consent). You will want to speak with a small group who provide unusual or interesting answers to the questions posed.

- Simplify the question set and use language that is universally understood.

- Avoid bias and loaded questions. Swinging the user in one direction as they're thinking through a response taints the entire exercise.

- Don't ask too many questions. The response quality and rate drops as the question base grows.

Additional UX research and information gathering methods

As we're only covering fundamentals, we won't have time to go over every single method of UX research. As a follow-up activity, I urge you to delve into the techniques below and find the right mix for your projects. You may find surveys ineffective, but usability testing highly effective for your purposes. Experiment, learn, and try again until you have a tried-and-true system.

- Usability Testing

- Eye Movement Tracking

- Field Study

- Card Sorting

- Storyboarding

- Heuristics

- Information Architecture

Accessibility

In the 1970s, Patricia Moore was frustrated and concerned. An industrial designer at a top design agency, Patricia was tasked with developing products for the masses. During a meeting, she asked her colleagues a question about simplifying refrigerator doors to cater to elderly users with arthritis. Expecting a positive response, Patricia was quickly shot down by a senior colleague who said "Patricia, we don't design for those people."

Dissatisfied and hurt, Patricia conducted a social experiment which involved dressing up as an old woman using prosthetics and makeup, and immersing herself in the life of an elderly citizen. What she found was truly remarkable. Products were not designed with the senior citizen population in mind, and tasks that were easy for her were putting a strain on this forgotten population of people.

At the conclusion of the study, Patricia approached design with a brand-new perspective and developed products that are universally usable. She's credited with inventing the rubber handle on kitchenware products (for improved grip) and pioneered the idea of "empathetic design".

So what's the lesson in all this?

Good product design isn't exclusionary. It's easy to de-prioritize accessibility in a fast-paced, make-and-break software development plan, but those who are on the margin are the ones who need the attention the most. Accessibility should be at the top of every product manager's priority list, and dedicating UX cycles to brainstorm solutions so 100 percent of the target audience is able to use the end product is mandatory in today's design thinking world.

Think like Patricia Moore.

Bad UX examples

Here are some particularly bad examples:

- Dark patterns: using greyed out or hard to click "X" or "Close" buttons. Hiding functionality is frustrating and if the user wants to leave, they will. Keep everything in plain sight.

- Infinite Scrolling: a continuous scroll on a web or mobile product can exude polish and slickness, but it's an abysmal experience for finding content hidden deep in view. If you have content that spans multiple refreshes, it's better to think up a new model for display to the end user.

- Liberal use of pop-up content: Pop-ups are slowly phasing their way out, but certain companies still use them to punch you in the face with ads or marketing content. The conversion uptick is not worth the friction, regardless of how subtle it is.

- Image carousels: Use of an image carousel is fun, but as with search results, people only pay attention to the first or second frame that is displayed. If you have content that requires user attention, a carousel isn't the ideal option of framing.

Identify your own in the software products you use, and think up ways in which the bad UX decision can be substituted to clear the path for user success while increasing conversion, engagement, or another desired metric for the organization.

Conclusion

A carefully planned and well-thought user experience is the holy grail for every product manager. Time is a non-renewable resource, and users don't want to spend it fumbling with your product to get what they need. Hire UX experts and designers, conduct research, and teach non-UXers about the importance of experience vs. aesthetic design. It will go a long way to acquiring loyal users for life (e.g., Apple).

■ ■ ■

CHAPTER 13

Industry Spotlight: Q&A with Leslie Shelton

Dr. Leslie Shelton, the Director of Product Development / Management at Elephant Ventures, created and manages the Product Manager discipline and the overall product development process at the company. She has a PhD from Brown University, where her focus was liquid crystal technology for bio-medical applications. She completed a postdoctoral position at the University of Hawaii's Queens Hospital, studying HIV-associated dementia, and completed a second postdoctoral position at Harvard Medical School, working at Children's Hospital in Boston where she studied chronic neuropathic pain in children. She later worked for DEKA R&D as a research scientist on water purification. Throughout her career as a scientist she was promoted to various roles in product development in mechanical, electrical, fluidics and software systems. She has been involved in all portions of the process including QA Tester, Engineer, Product Owner, and her current role as Director of Product Development.

What does the term "product manager" mean to you?

The Product Manager role can vary greatly. I recently developed the practice for my company. After compiling a comprehensive package of process documents, templates, and role descriptions, I wanted to add a brief high-level outline of the major activities, that if done well, would provide a high likelihood of success. Here is that list of activities:

1. The Problem and Thought Leadership: The PM must understand the problem statement. What is this product trying to solve and for whom? The PM should continually evaluate the solution against these inputs and focus on prioritizing what brings the most business value.

2. The big picture: Once a solution has been chosen, prior to the engineering engagement, the PM should map the full scope of work. It should be defined with enough rigor and detail that the engineers can create DB models and the product architecture. This will keep the work focused and uncover a roadmap of decisions, dependencies, and integration points to be worked out during development.

3. The little picture: With a strong solution scope, the PM should start at the top of the priority list and work their way down adding complete clarity and definition to each feature. The PM should stay in front of the engineers so by the time they get to a feature, they can develop it without any ambiguity or lingering requirements questions.

4. Unblock: Always be unblocking. The content in the two previous bullets will naturally uncover blockers. PMs must quickly locate the source of the block and reach out immediately as needed to the appropriate persons. If the current approach isn't doable, the PM will determine what are the alternate options and choose the best path forward.

5. Budget: PMs should always be aware of the current and projected budget. In agile, the scope and roadmaps are ever-evolving based on stakeholder feedback and the effects on budget should be kept in sight.

What is the best way to rebound from failure as a PM?

Rebounding from a PM failure is like rebounding from any other. One must be able to be introspective without ego. If there is enough self-awareness to locate failure points, one can outline the mitigation plan, make the appropriate process updates, and start again. It isn't about the product manager. It is about the product.

How has your background contributed to your success as a PM?

Because I've done all aspects of product development from starting with a problem and devising a solution, prototyping, development, trials, user testing, and market strategy, I am familiar with all parts of the process.

My physics background has helped me with organizing my work, solving problems, and being extremely diligent. PMs are not fly-by management. They need to be able to see the big picture and dive into the details.

How would you go about hiring product managers on your team? Any specific skills that you'd look for?

In hiring PMs, I look for the following skills:

Diligence – If the PM doesn't know the tiny details, who does?

Sense of urgency – PMs set the mood and the pace of the project. There shouldn't be stress--it's a fun role(!)--but they should operate with velocity.

Lack of ego – This will help make the environment transparent and the faster PMs can admit mistakes, the faster they can course-correct.

Multi-tasker – In a project environment, problems don't come up in an orderly fashion. PMs must be able to juggle and disseminate new information, prioritize, and lead the team through the evolving roadmap. Project needs are what set the work and schedule.

Good Instincts - Everyone can be trained to be a better manager but there are those who have better managerial instincts. While knowledge of a given field is extremely valuable, I've found more success with those who have the right instincts about what to focus on and what questions to ask. Without intimate knowledge of the product, those with better instincts can still know where to obtain the necessary information and still make the right decisions for the product.

Can you give us an example of one of your favorite products and why?

I really enjoy my work, so every project becomes my favorite while I am doing it. However, the phase of projects I most appreciate is in the beginning during problem refinement and solution ideation. I like to help solve challenging problems and use creativity. An example was a medical application where a hospital was the customer, nurses were the users, and patients were ultimately the recipients of the technology. Their "asks" were quite different and seemingly conflicting. It was a great accomplishment to strategize a solution that added value across the various stakeholders and would make an impact on healthcare – particularly for resource-limited patients.

What's your approach for defining a long-term product strategy?

In defining a long-term product strategy, it is important to take frequent intermissions to re-evaluate the long-term goals and solution. In order to do this, our approach has been incremental steps with clear business value. First, you complete a handful of key features, test them, make necessary updates, then re-evaluate the problem and solution. Based on your evaluation, you pick the next key features and set up for the following round.

How do you coordinate the balance between product and engineering?

I don't! I step through each task in priority order and fulfill the needs that emerge. The work itself dictates the appropriate balance between product and engineering.

CHAPTER 14

■ ■ ■

Rapid Prototyping

"The problem with prototypes is that they don't always work"

— Laurie Anderson

Human beings are visual creatures. The shiny new MacBook, glossy new sports car, or rare designer apparel instantly capture our attention. A product manager may have a crystal-clear idea of what the product looks like in their head even before formal design is kicked off, but it's tough to communicate the vision to management or the team. If the team you're on doesn't have budget for a UI / UX designer before the software development cycle is kicked off, the product manager will absorb the responsibility of coming up with rough sketches of the end deliverable. Many of my PM colleagues don't want to touch design tools like Balsamiq or Sketch because they fear it will require too much commitment to learn, but this chapter is designed to ramp you up to these software tools quickly so you can externalize your creativity in a short period of time. The wireframes and mocks aren't expected to be world class, but it helps to supply mocks that act as a north star for the team so everyone is aligned on the draft form and function. Prototyping a tool can persuade stakeholders early in a way that words on a page can't, and we'll guide you through just enough of the features and functionality of industry-leading tools to craft a presentable wireframe or mock.

What is rapid prototyping?

Rapid prototyping is a usability practice that involves forming a hypothesis on a product that will solve a problem, then developing a cheap and rough prototype (interactive or physical) to test with users for early feedback. Rapid prototyping can take many forms, starting with paper prototypes sketched out on notepads all the way to fully-fleshed out mocks using Sketch or Photoshop. Create a visual UI, record how users interact with the tool to test assumptions, then recreate the UI over and over again until it reaches a ready state for implementation.

© Aswin Pranam 2018
A. Pranam, *Product Management Essentials*, https://doi.org/10.1007/978-1-4842-3303-0_14

Why should we create prototypes?

Reasons for creating prototypes are:

- **Early user involvement:** user (both internal and external) eyes on an early-stage version of the product sets to tone for success down the line. Laying out a paper prototype and having them fake "click" on screens or provide feedback on critical or unnecessary features can influence prioritization of the backlog, and sometimes change the initial design entirely.

- **Cheap:** it costs nothing in the long run to fire up a wireframing tool or draw out the concept ideas. Before investing hundreds of thousands on a near-final UI, start with a stripped-down version and iterate from there.

- **Compatible with Agile:** prototype, test, rinse, and repeat. A prototype can go through several revisions before it's accepted as the best solution, which directly ties into the core ethos of agile development.

- **Enables A / B testing of proposed UIs:** team members' hypotheses can be tested in parallel by showing one version of the prototype to a set of users and another version to a second representative group.

- **Observable user feedback:** in a user research or focus group setting, you can assign the roles of moderator and observer to members of the product team. This way, one member will walk the user through the prototype while the other records every observation and notes takeaways.

- **More opportunities for creative risk:** out-of-the-box ideas can be integrated into the prototype without any repercussions or risk.

- **Opens up the design process to entire team:** any team member with an opinion can contribute without feeling like design is siloed just to the designers.

Low-fidelity vs. high-fidelity vs. mocks vs. interactive prototypes

Before we proceed to mocking up UI frames, we need to accept a set of definitions. There's a lot of subjectivity around what constitutes a low-fidelity prototype versus high-fidelity, and the level of interactivity required for a mock to fall into the interactive prototype bucket. For this book, we'll standardize the terms in the following way:

- **Low-fidelity:** anything sketched on a notepad, napkin, or similar medium. Basic UI sketched as a jumping off point for later revision.

- **High-fidelity:** often referred to as **wireframes**, high-fidelity UIs are drafted up using web tools such as Balsamiq. Wireframes contain feature details and multiple screens to establish a user flow.

- **Mock:** full visually featured UI frames with color, fonts, styling, and icons included. Everything is complete, aside from actual live functionality.

- **Interactive Prototype:** a mock tied together using a prototyping tool like InVision. Interactive prototypes can be clicked and interacted with. Features will either work completely or provide simulated feedback to mimic a real interface.

High-fidelity UI development with Balsamiq

Balsamiq is a fast web and desktop wireframing tool released in 2008. It's widely used in corporate America and startupland, and is the #1 choice among product managers that I know for UI development. It's useful for wireframing any type of web or mobile product, and contains a rich portfolio of icons, shapes, and settings to mold the right UI. The first-run UIs developed with Balsamiq can act as a shell for a mock by a designer, or it can be thrown into a PowerPoint in sequential order to demonstrate early product functionality to stakeholders.

In this section, we'll use Balsamiq to create an inspired clone of Todoist, a popular to-do list app. To demonstrate how easy and accessible Balsamiq is for wireframing, I'll build the high-fidelity UI in under 30 minutes. If you're able, follow along as you read the instructions. That's all the time it takes to produce a usable set of UI frames to take to the user.

To begin, let's take a look at the mobile view of the Todoist application (Figure 14-1).

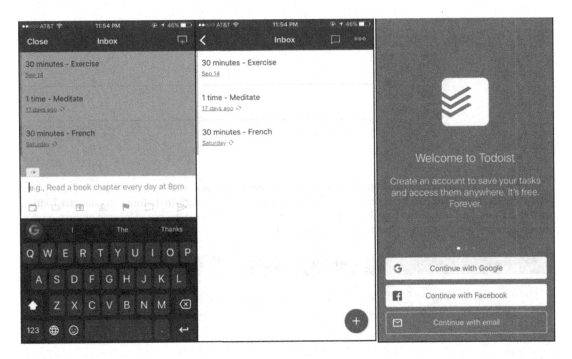

Figure 14-1. *The mobile view*

Figure 14-2 shows the web view of the Todoist application.

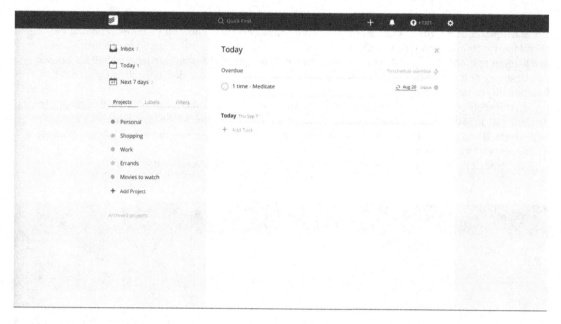

Figure 14-2. *The web view*

Navigate to Balsamiq.com and open the web demo version. Balsamiq allows first-timers to trial the product in hourly blocks, so it's a good way to get your feet wet with the platform before you purchase (which I highly recommend). Once the page loads, you'll see a grid-view, with a master panel located at the top with buttons, shapes, text, and other elements you can use to build the

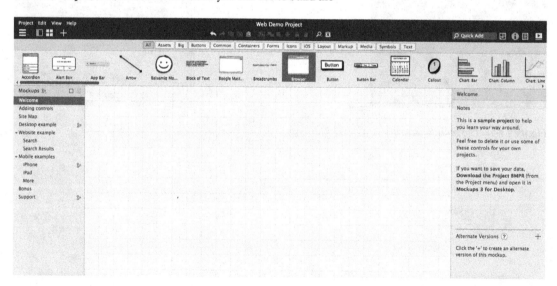

Drag the "Browser" element into the middle of the screen and resize it to match the dimensions shown in Figure 14-3. Then, choose a blank Rectangle element, drag it into the Browser, and use the corners to create a slim bar sitting directly under the grey header of the browser. Use the tools panel on the right-hand side to change the background color of the bar from white to black.

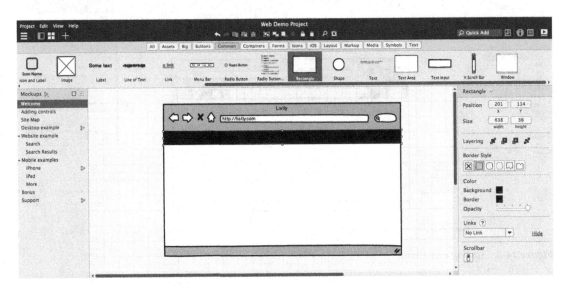

Figure 14-3. *Starting our UI design*

Use the search bar on the top right hand corner to look up icons to add to our design. At this stage, search for "logo" and "search box". Drag the icons into the displayed positions on top of the black bar (Figure 14-4).

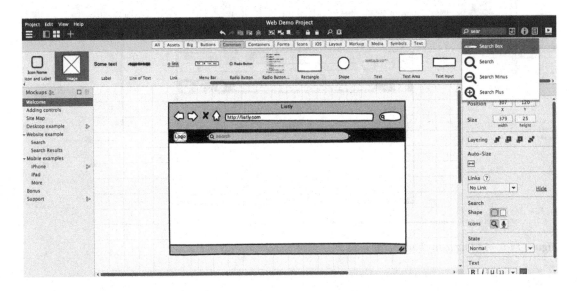

Figure 14-4. *Adding a search box and logo*

Continue adding icons to the bar by searching for "bell", "light bulb", and "cogs" (Figure 14-5).

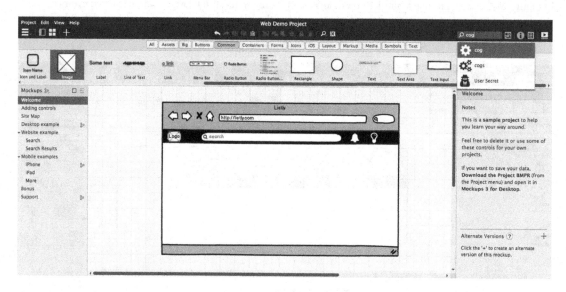

Figure 14-5. Adding more icons

Now that the header panel is complete, let's switch focus to the body of the page. Pull down the "Label" element, copy and paste it three times, and rename the labels to "Inbox", "Today", and "Next 7 Days". Once this is done, search for the "inbox" and "calendar" icons to decorate the left side of the labels (Figure 14-6).

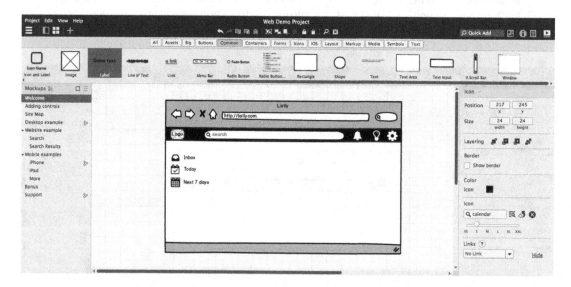

Figure 14-6. Adding to the body of the page

Next, drag four circular shapes from the "Common" tab on the elements panel. Click on each one individually to surface the tools bar, and color them accordingly: red, purple, blue, and green. Then, copy and paste four more "Label" elements and name the circles Personal, Shopping, Work, and Errands. You'll notice we also have a grey background effect to accompany the left panel. To do this, color a "Rectangle" element grey, use the "Layering" setting on the tools panel once selecting, and choose the option to send the rectangle to the back. Finally, change the background color of the rectangle to light grey and experiment with the Opacity setting until it matches Figure 14-7.

Figure 14-7. *Adding a grey background effect*

To finish up, drag "Label" elements and change the text to match the wireframe in Figure 14-8. Use the tools panel on the right to change the text size. Then, use the circle shape element to create four identical circles, and experiment with the border setting of each to create a bold outer rim.

Figure 14-8. *Adding more labels*

That's all it takes. We now have a web wireframe for our to-do list app. Now, let's move onto developing a set of wireframes for a mobile view.

Clear the grid view by selecting all the elements and hitting "Delete" on your keyboard. Then, select the "iOS" tab from the top panel and drag three iPhone elements into the body of the page, side-by-side as shown in Figure 14-9.

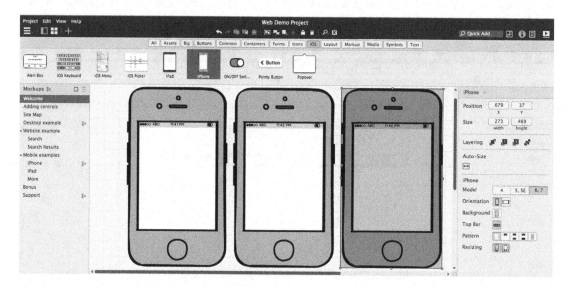

Figure 14-9. *Theree iPhones in a row*

Drag a "Rectangle" element into the first iPhone, along with a "Label" element changed to "Listly" and a check mark icon found using the search bar. Next, use the search bar to find the icons for login, sign up, and Google. Align the icons under the logo box, and use labels to tag the icons appropriately (Figure 14-10).

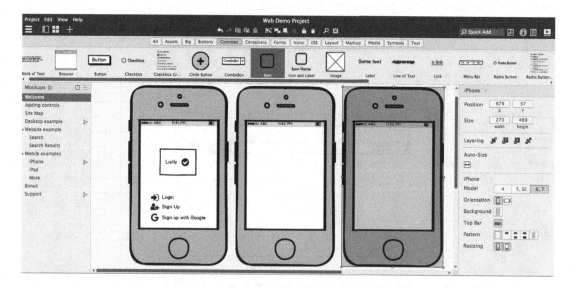

Figure 14-10. *Populating the first iPhone screen*

Next is the "create a task" screen (Figure 14-11). Under the "iOS" tab, you'll find an element for the entire keyboard. Drag this into the second screen, along with the flag, tag, and arrow icons. Then, drag text to the top of the screen, change the color to light grey, and replace the default text with "Type in your task..."

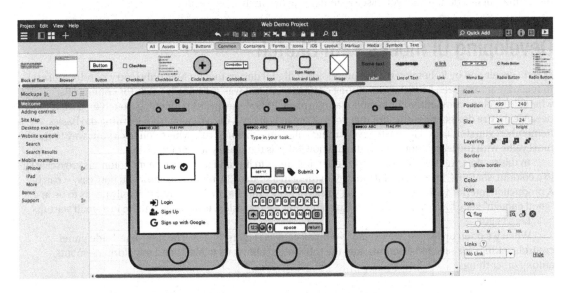

Figure 14-11. *Building the "create a task" screen*

Finish by putting together the "list view" of the to-do app (Figure 14-12). Try to see if you can figure out how the frame is built without explicit instruction.

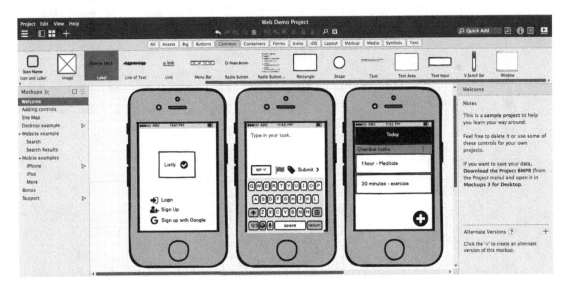

Figure 14-12. *Adding a list view to the third screen*

Pat yourself on the back, you've created a set of wireframes in a very short amount of time! By now, you've started to develop mental patterns on how UIs can be pulled together fast, and the concept of reusable elements is firmly engrained in your mind. Using components previously developed by others are the bedrock of fast design, and you'll see a similar practice in the next section.

Developing UI mocks with Sketch

Sketch, developed by Bohemian BV, is a professional digital design tool for Mac only (sorry Windows users). In recent years, it's been a fan favorite among designers since it was specifically made for crafting UIs, whereas the close competitor Photoshop is all-purpose. PMs shy away from touching Sketch or similar tools because they're designer-centric, but that doesn't mean you can't derive value from learning the basics. Remember: you don't need to master everything. Following an 80/20 rule where you hack your way to the most value with the least amount of in-depth knowledge is the place you want to be in.

In this section, we'll use Sketch to bring our wireframes to life, and take it from a monotonous greyscale UI to a colorful, sharp UI. Like before, I'll build everything in a span of 30 minutes to show you how easy it can be. A production interface will have weeks upon weeks of work done before it's ready, but it only needs to be in a "good enough" state for a product manager to communicate the vision, especially if you're in a small startup.

Let's begin!

When we open up Sketch, we're lead to a blank canvas (Figure 14-13). The right-hand side panel controls settings for selected elements, and the top toolbar allows us to insert and transform elements, among other things.

Figure 14-13. *The opening screen of Sketch*

Since we're developing a web application, we can generate artboards by selecting File ➤ New from Template ➤ Web Design (Figure 14-14). For other types of apps, we'd choose a different template. After the click, you'll see a variety of small canvas views for desktop, tablet, and mobile views.

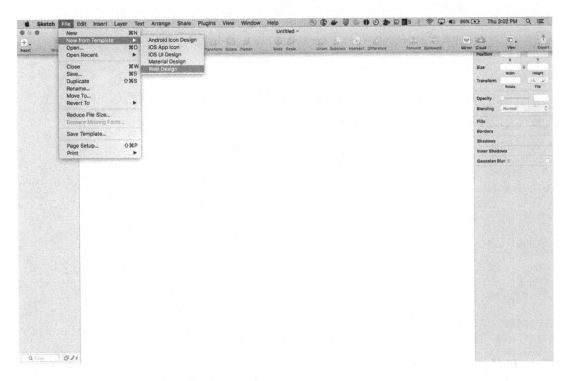

Figure 14-14. *Selecting a web application template*

Before we begin mocking up the core application, let's design a simple logo. Start by selecting Insert ➤ Shape ➤ Rounded.

Figure 14-15. *Selecting the logo shape*

Using the tool, draw out a logo with 400 X 400 dimensions.

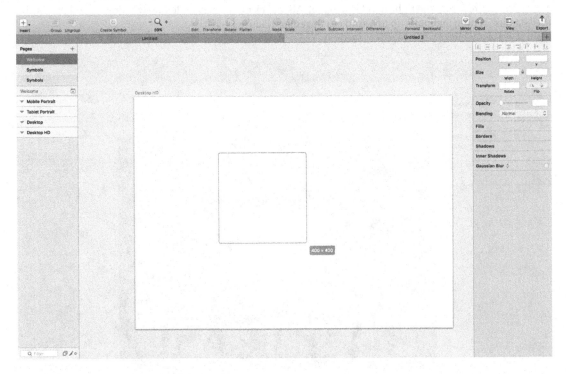

Figure 14-16. *Drawing the logo shape*

Once the logo is drawn out, click on the "Desktop HD" section in the left-hand side panel under "Welcome". This will bring up settings for the Desktop HD artboard, and you'll be able to change the background to red from the right-hand side panel. Also, click on the rectangle that was drawn, and play with the "Radius" setting that pops up to round out the edges (Figure 14-17).

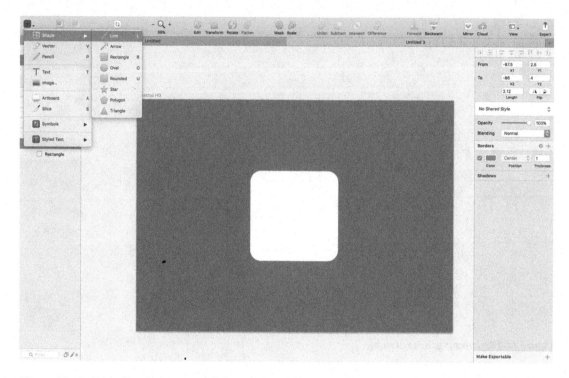

Figure 14-17. *Rounding the corners and choosing a red background*

Use Insert ➤ Shape ➤ Line to create a horizontal bar (change fill to red). Then, drag this bar across the top half of the rectangle (Figure 14-18).

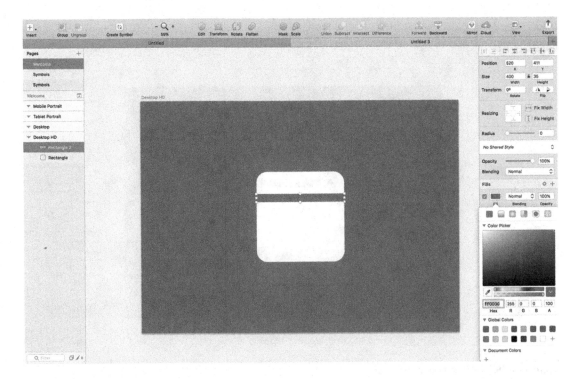

Figure 14-18. *Adding a horizontal bar*

Click Insert ➤ Shape ➤ Rectangle to add 15 grey rectangles to the logo (Figure 14-19).

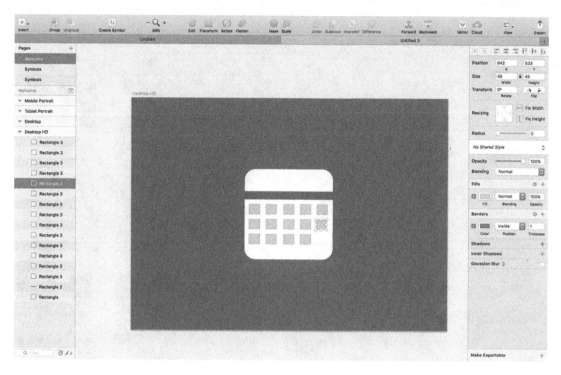

Figure 14-19. *Adding grey rectangles*

At this point, all of the individual components you assembled into the logo are separate. This can get annoying if you want to treat them all as one singular logo. To group the components into a single element, select all of them from the left-hand side panel, right-click, and select "Group Selection" (Figure 14-20).

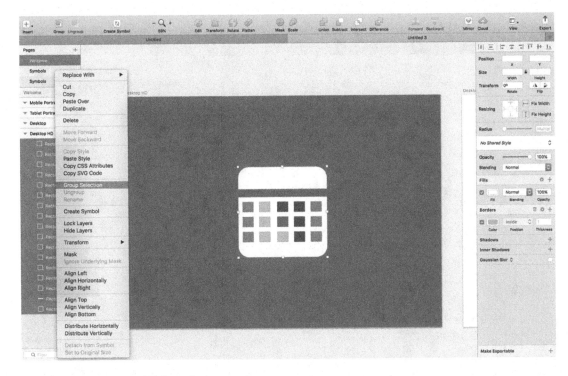

Figure 14-20. Grouping the logo elements

Now that the logo is complete, let's redirect our attention back to the web application. Open a new Sketch template, and use a set of three rectangles (Insert ➤ Shape ➤ Rectangle) to create a grey top panel, and two light grey shaded rectangles on the left and right side by resizing and changing the fill (Figure 14-21).

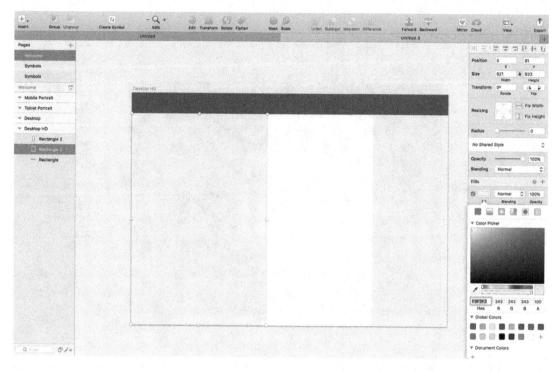

Figure 14-21. *Adding three rectangles to the web application*

Select Insert ➤ Text to add a header. Rename the default to "Today" (Figure 14-22).

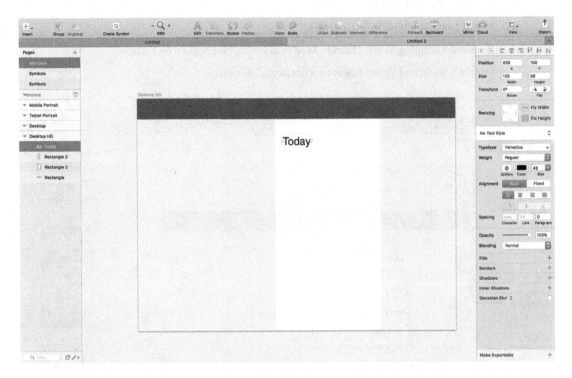

Figure 14-22. *Adding a header*

As shown in Figure 14-23, using a combination of shapes and text, decorate the left panel with:

- Inbox, Today, and Next 7 Days labels
- 5 ovals (red, grey, blue, green, purple)
- Personal, Shopping, Work, Errands, Movies to watch, and Add Project labels
- Project, Labels, and Filters labels on a horizontal line shape

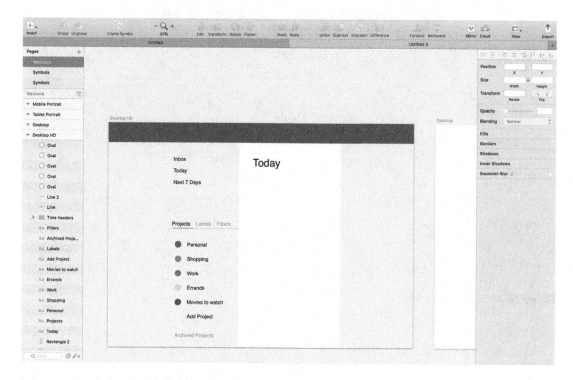

Figure 14-23. *Decorating the left panel*

To create the visual indicator of Projects being underlined in the UI, we can add a second line to the artboard, color it a shade of grey darker using the tools panel, and drag the line (in this case, Line 2) above the original line so it sits above (Figure 14-24).

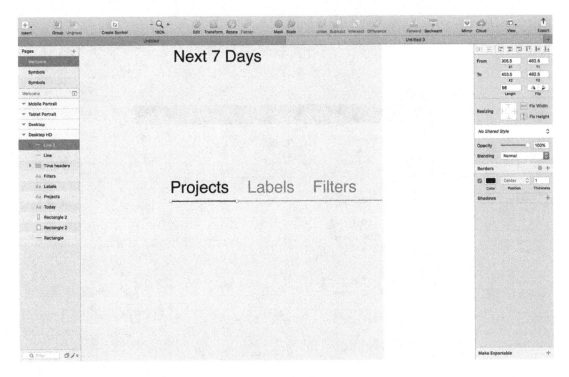

Figure 14-24. *Adding a visual cue for Projects*

Following similar design patterns, use a combination of text, lines, and oval shapes to create a to-do task item under "Today". Then, group the task item shapes together into a group called "Line Item" (Figure 14-25). This allows us to copy paste new line items without having to redo the effort each time.

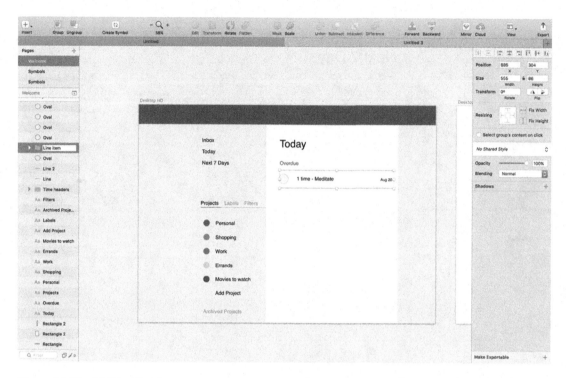

Figure 14-25. *Adding a line item*

Copy & paste the "Line Item" group twice to create two new tasks, and add text for "Today", "Thu Sept 7", and "Add Task" with a single line separator (Figure 14-26).

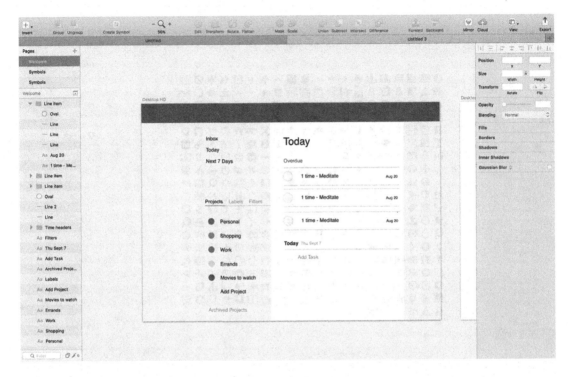

Figure 14-26. *Filling in more line items*

For icons, Sketch doesn't come with pre-installed packages like Balsamiq. However, we can do a simple web search and come up with tons of free, open-source Sketch UI kits that are available for use. We'll use icons from Font Awesome for our purposes (Figure 14-27).

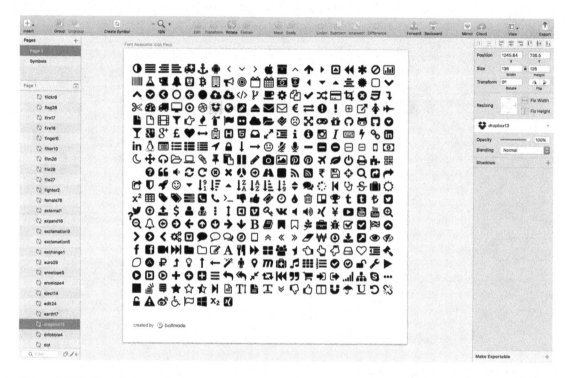

Figure 14-27. *Font Awesome fonts*

The final step is to copy icons from the Font Awesome set, and add them in the missing spots (Figure 14-28).

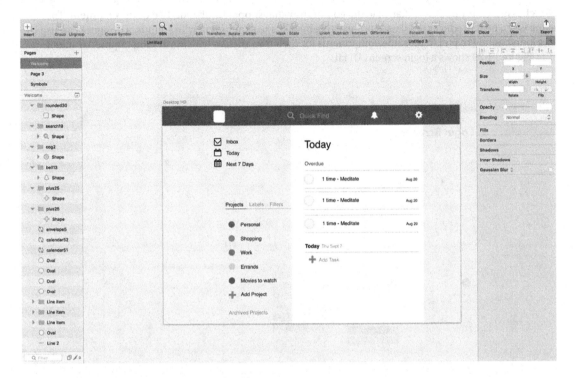

Figure 14-28. *Adding the Font Awesome icons*

A web application view, delivered in 30 minutes or less.

Example #1: Login screens UI kit

Sketch is incredibly powerful thanks to the community that supports collaborative UI development. The same way a beat producer or DJ uses pre-existing beat kits to experiment with sounds, a designer can use UI kits found online to pull in reusable components for their own mocks, with attribution required if stated.

Figure 14-29 shows a login screens UI kit.

Figure 14-29. *Login screens UI kit*

Example #2: Analytics dashboard UI kit

Figure 14-30 shows an analytics dashboard UI kit.

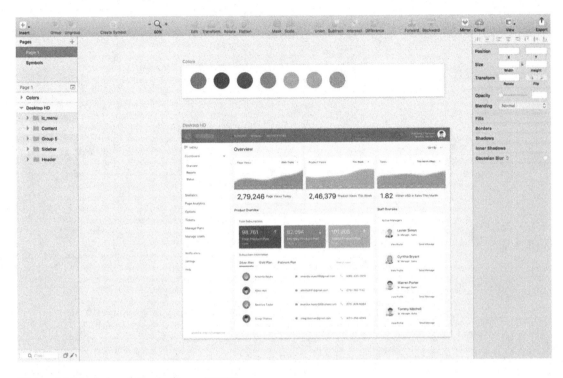

Figure 14-30. *An analytics dashboard UI kit*

Conclusion

Throughout this chapter, we covered prototyping at a high level, walked through the benefits of rapid prototyping, and created wireframes and mocks using Balsamiq and Sketch. Practice refining the habit of mocking UIs quickly before throwing resources at the problem. Begin with cheap, rough, and incomplete. Then, move forward as confidence in the product grows.

CHAPTER 15

■ ■ ■

The Good, The Bad, and The Unusable

"Knowing how people will use something is essential"

— Don Norman

If you haven't had the pleasure of reading "The Design of Everyday Things" by Don Norman, stop what you're doing, fire up your Amazon account, and go purchase it. If you're turned off at the thought of adding yet another book to your growing reading list, the visual learners should check out Tony Fadell's TED talk titled "The first secret of design is...noticing". Why all of the recommendations?

Because I want you to care about how your product looks, feels, and operates.

Plenty of times throughout your PM career, you'll be tasked with building a product that is unsexy and bland at the surface. It could be an HR application, internal developer portal, or proof-of-concept scheduler, but you'll approach it with the enthusiasm of a college student taking the SATs. After all, you have to take a couple losses early in your career so you can work on flying cars, artificially intelligent robots, and other cooler projects later on, right?

Wrong.

A PM can take any mundane software offering and turn it into a product that delights the end user. Workday (an HR application) is a friendly, bright platform that takes the guesswork out of payroll and employee / benefits information. Salesforce (a customer relationship management platform) innovated by taking a space crowded with monolithic platforms and moved the practice of managing client contacts into the cloud. Countless examples exist of applications that maneuvered a boring space and found a way to differentiate themselves, creating a billion-dollar company in the process.

As users, we also develop an emotional attachment to the products we use daily. For example, how many times have you been in a debate with a team member or peer about the following products?

JIRA vs. Pivotal Tracker

Trello vs. Asana

Sublime Text vs. Atom

iOS vs. Android

The end user is highly impressionable when new products hit the market, and your job is to identify the latest trends, forecast a user's needs, and cater to them in the simplest, most straightforward fashion. In this chapter, I'll walk you through a handful of good, bad, and unusable products, both in the realm of technology and elsewhere. I want you to pay attention to the small points of friction, areas of improvement, moments of delight, and overall user experience the product is meant to deliver to the customer. Interweave form and function into an intuitive and functionally sound product, and the user's hearts will be won forever (or at least until the next big thing comes along).

© Aswin Pranam 2018
A. Pranam, *Product Management Essentials*, https://doi.org/10.1007/978-1-4842-3303-0_15

The Good

Let's start with the good examples.

The Bradley Timepiece

At my core, my sense of materialism extends to three distinct products: watches, shoes, and sunglasses. I grew up wearing Timex and Swatch timepieces with quartz movements, and quickly graduated to automatic movements once I realized how they were assembled and operated. Last year, when I was perusing the exhibits at the Red Dot Design Museum in Singapore, the Bradley watch immediately caught my eye (www.eone-time.com and Figure 15-1). The titanium finish coupled with a mesh band stood out unlike any timepiece I've ever seen, and the way it sat behind the glass enclosure made me say "I need to get this". Beyond just the aesthetics that differentiate this timepiece from others on the market, the true product win is the attention paid to accessibility. If you look closely, there's no minute, second, or hour hand. Instead, the Bradley uses two magnetic ball bearings, one on the inner circle and one on the outer edge as a marker for time. You may be thinking "well, that's a bit annoying. It doesn't lend itself well to telling time quickly."

Figure 15-1. *The Bradley timepiece (image courtesy Scott Schiller, https://www.flickr.com/photos/schill/, under CC-BY license)*

That's what blind users have been struggling with for 99% of watches on the market. With the Bradley, it's easy to identify the elevated hour and minute markers, and a swift touch across the surface and sides of the watch can help a blind user tell the time with ease. No fuss, no extra bells and whistles. Just a user interface that works.

What's so special about it?

The folks at Eone (parent company) managed to ship a product that appeals to the masses while still hitting a target market that desperately needed a way to tell time. Traditional watches are usually restrictive to blind users since their time indicators are hidden behind a cased enclosure, but the exposed nature of the Bradley perfectly caters to accessibility users without sacrificing on design.

Key takeaway

Often times, when running through a development lifecycle for a software product, accessibility is left on the backburner. The 80/20 principle is applied to optimizing everything, and PMs tend to ignore users who fall in the category of an edge case. As a leader who is responsible for prioritizing and pushing features, PMs usually bake in hard features instead of finding ways to make the existing product easier to use for everyone because time is a limited resource. The Bradley fundamentally rejects the principle that accessibility is an afterthought, and puts it front-and-center as a value proposition for buying this product in a sea of thousands of competing products.

Early prototype vehicle - Waymo

Self-driving cars, once fully realized, will change every aspect of our society, from transportation, to urban design, productivity, consumer safety, and reallocation of empty space. The engineers at Waymo (Google), Tesla, and traditional auto manufacturers have their work cut out for them, but early indications and tests show that the technology will eventually succeed and be usable for urban and suburban environments alike. The thought of lounging back and getting work done on a driverless trip from San Francisco to Los Angeles sounds like a dream come true for me, but people across the United States who don't trust technology approach the topic with a healthy dose of skepticism.

And why wouldn't they?

People love being in control of their own destiny, and handing the wheel to a million plus lines of code can be unsettling to many. That's why, for the first iteration of the self-driving car prototype demoed for the public, Google pulled a genius move. Instead of wiring up a standard sedan or SUV with dozens of sensors and exposed cameras on the exterior, they designed a car that looks cute and approachable (Figure 15-2).

Figure 15-2. *The first Waymo car (image courtesy of* `www.waymo.com/press/`*)*

What's so special about it?

If I ask you to think of adjectives to describe a motor vehicle, you may respond with keywords like "sleek", "torque", "horsepower", "fast", and "safe". Stripping away the first impressions, we're left with a metal death trap that is a result of engineering, metal forming, polymers, industrial labor, and strict manufacturing processes. Understanding that users may see the first iteration in a negative light if it represented what they already knew, Google turned the idea on its head and delivered a car unlike anything we've ever seen. It caught people off guard, and although plenty mocked and laughed at the cute nature of the vehicle, nobody saw it as a threat. It lowered the defenses of the future end user, and tore through their initial misconceptions.

Key takeaway

Find ways to downplay the fears of the user. We have entire industries built on fear (or the avoidance of bad things happening), so leveraging creative ways to put the customer at ease so they can see the product for what it truly is can be a powerful tool in a PMs arsenal during the design process.

Square Cash app

Scenario: I'm at a bar with one of my close friends Ron, and I left my wallet at home. He ends up paying for drinks the entire night, and I feel bad that he has to pick up the tab each time. Luckily, I have a smartphone with the Cash app instead. So I fire it up, and see the interface in Figure 15-3.

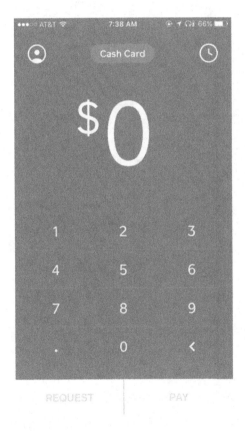

Figure 15-3. *The opening screen*

To settle the balance, I press ($)1 on the keypad (Figure 15-4) and hit "PAY" at the bottom right hand corner. (Let's assume we're in a cheap part of the world where an entire night's worth of drinks only total $1.)

Figure 15-4. *$1 entered*

I'm led to an account selector screen, where I click on Ron's name, along with an explanation for the fund transfer in the "For" row (Figure 15-5). Lastly, I hit "PAY" again in the upper-right-hand corner.

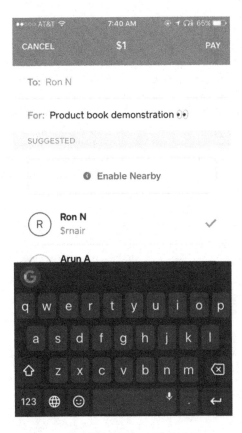

Figure 15-5. *Selecting the recipient*

And viola, $1 was sent to Ron (Figure 15-6). The funds will immediately be deposited into his linked bank account without any further action on his part.

Figure 15-6. Confirmation

The Cash app is minimalism at its finest. French writer Antoine de Saint-Exupery once said "perfection is achieved, not when there is nothing more to add, but when there is nothing left to take away," and the Cash app is the digital embodiment of that statement. Short, sweet, and to the point. No extra fluff or features required. In a space as complicated and difficult as peer-to-peer payments, Square managed to reduce the friction on the user end and deliver an experience that immediately locks you into the app.

What's so special about it?

For the general population, splitting checks and paying others back is a headache that comes with life. Until Cash (or Venmo) was invented, the painstaking process of deciding who takes the check and how the bill will be repaid was a conversation everyone wanted to avoid. With Cash, the payment can be sent and received on the spot, and the burden of collection no longer falls on the sponsor of the purchase.

Also, Square's signup flow is painless. Sign in, link a bank account, and never worry about it again. When you reopen the application, there's no need to re-authenticate yourself since you're using a trusted device, and you can send payments faster than the service worker walks to the table with the bill.

Fun fact: According to a story published by The Verge, the first run version of Cash was designed after Jack Dorsey (Square CEO) told the creative director to walk through the Museum of Modern Art for inspiration.

Key takeaway

Every UI frame in an appflow is a potential drop-off point for the user. I can't tell you how many apps I've abandoned because one button press resulted in lost progress, or the sign up took longer than it needed to. Collect the bare minimum, and let the product fall in the hands of the user as fast as possible. Abstract away the complexities of the application, and don't let a moment of frustration result in a user moving away from you to a capable competitor.

The Bad

Now it's time for the bad.

Hotel shower handle (Wroclaw, Poland)

Note: I live in sunny Palo Alto, California, and the shower handle discussed in this section doesn't fit the mental model I have of how shower handles work in general. However, European bathroom design standards are not an area I'm well-versed in, so if this is a common and intuitive way of building controls overseas, apologies in advance and pardon my ignorance. Still, good design should be universal, so I'll continue to complain aggressively.

After a long, grueling day of travel, all I want to do is relax with a long, warm shower. I step into the booth and come face-to-face with what appears to be a standard shower setting (Figure 15-7).

Figure 15-7. *First impression*

As I look closer, all I see is a long chrome tube with a blank circular knob. No hot/cold settings, no visual affordance to guide me in the right direction. I started to turn the end of the knob, hoping this will kick things off (Figure 15-8).

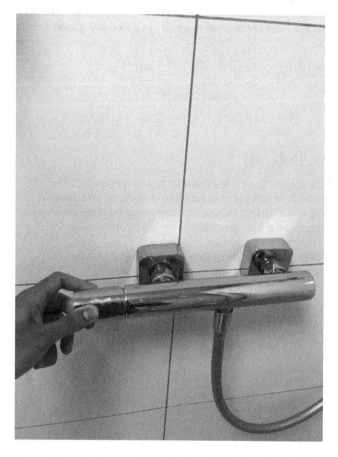

Figure 15-8. *Turning the knob*

Nope.
Next, I attempt to pull the knob towards me, hoping this is the correct action.
Nope.
Frustrated, I start turning the knob, covering multiple full revolutions in both directions.
Still nothing.

I was all but ready to lose my mind until I realized the knob curved on a hinge when pushed inward (Figure 15-9). This simultaneously affected the pressure of the water as well (the more I pushed it in, the more water came out).

Figure 15-9. *Movement at last*

OK. Progress, but the lack of a hot / cold setting left me fumbling with the knob, turning it in both directions until I finally reached my desired temperature.

What ruined the user experience?

Shower handles / faucet levers have to be one of the most poorly designed inventions of all time. My suspicion is that there's a secret collective of industrial designers who all get together once a year to brainstorm ways to piss people off and make them fumble around with the preferences until they eventually give up and settle (sorry, I'm passionate about a relaxing shower). In my scenario, the desire for a full, all-chrome-everything pattern prevented the designer from adding what matters the most: visual assistance to operate the knob. Even after I understood the action required to reach the end goal, I struggled to get the pressure and temperature precisely where I wanted it to be.

Key Takeaway

Don't sacrifice utility for consistency. Adding a couple icons or red/blue lining could have saved the experience. Making the user think about what they need to do instead of it being handled subsciously is a sign of product shortcoming.

Confusing street signs

Since we covered design failures for our neighbors across the pond, it's only fair to bring the same level of scrutiny back home to the United States. In any densely populated city center, parking is a mess and our urban epicenters are no different. Paying outrageous fees for covered parking is one strategy, but avoiding the exorbitant price comes at the cost of risking a tow. Why? Because street signs can be downright confusing half the time (Figure 15-10). In cases where multiple signs occupy a single outpost, the user spends valuable time calculating a schedule in their head based on an overload of information. Certain cities across the United States have tested new methods of displaying the information which has proven to be effective, but legacy signs still remain and they can throw you off if you're not careful or attentive.

Figure 15-10. *A jumble of signs*

What ruins the user experience?

Stressing the user out when they're one step away from their final destination isn't ideal. Distill the message down only to what the human on the receiving end of the message cares about. Personally, I don't care if it's street cleaning or a six-month parade; just tell me when I can park and when I can't.

Key Takeaway

Don't make the end user think. Less brain processing for the day-to-day minutiae so we can save it for moments that matter.

The Unusable

Finally, the unusable.

(Bad) Digital Advertising

> *"The best minds of my generation are thinking about how to make people click ads. That sucks."*
>
> — Jeffrey Hammerbacher

Digital advertising, in the general sense, is broken from a user value standpoint. Around the globe, over 10%+ of users are actively using ad-blocking software to clear advertisements from their browser, and mobile ad-blocking rates continue to climb. On one hand, you could argue that in exchange for using a free product or service on the Internet, the price you pay is a couple seconds of your attention for a floating banner or video advertisement. That's a fair and reasonable point of view to hold.

However, the nature of digital advertising has ruined the web and mobile experience for so many users that winning their trust back is difficult (or damn near impossible). I've flatly refused to download apps in the past that contain full screen ads or repeat the same ad content over and over again in the hopes that I eventually click through (Note: repetition will NOT cause me to magically want the product over time). Great products can unknowingly add a black mark to their reputation by inserting ads carelessly. Every single element of the product tells a piece of the complete story, and ad placement needs to be handled with care.

How can we do better?

Advertising is the lifeblood of an overwhelming majority of web and mobile companies, and the paradigm of app-based monetization is here to stay, at least for the foreseeable future. When integrating ads into your product, follow a few key principles:

- Ads should be nonintrusive, and blend with adjacent elements on the screen. If a user is scrolling and naturally passes an advertisement, they're less likely to be ticked off than if they are smacked in the face with an interstitial that halts the natural flow.

- Don't collect a ton of user data upfront for later stage advertising. People are starting to open their eyes to the realities of sharing data to third parties online, and overcollection can drive privacy conscious users away.

- Don't use UI dark patterns to artificially inflate conversion rates. An "X" button that matches the background color of the banner or only activates after Y seconds is a bad, bad move. I, along with the rest of universe, pledge to bombard your app reviews with one star if this is caught in the wild.

An example of subtle yet effective ad placement is shown below for the "Be Focused" macOS application (Figure 15-11). It hangs as a panel on the footer of the frame, and I notice it every time I click into the application without being annoyed or burdened.

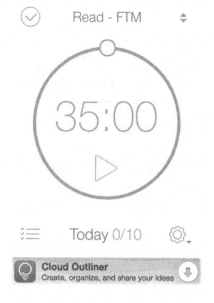

Figure 15-11. *The Be Focused UI*

Good advertising is something users desperately need. When your favorite artist drops a new album, you want to receive an ad alerting you about its existence. If the new season of Game of Thrones drops, you want your TV to pop up with a banner telling you the exciting news. This may not seem like advertising, but the entire goal of the industry is to communicate a message to sell a product, service, or idea. As creatures of consumerist culture, we're constantly on the lookout for the latest and greatest to improve our lives, and advertising can be a tool to satisfy our need if done correctly.

■ ■ ■

CHAPTER 16

Industry Spotlight: Q&A with Daniel Csonth

Prior to joining McKinsey, Daniel was the first Product Manager hire at a travel tech startup that he helped scale up rapidly with his product and strategy insights. He implemented state of the art Agile practices, broadened the product portfolio, and refocused the business on SaaS centered around conversational interactions - a new, emerging paradigm of user experience. Elsewhere, Daniel has been a Product Manager in a range of environments with a successful track record in early stage innovation, product launches and finding product-market-fit.

What does the term product manager mean to you?

To me, being a Product Manager means the ability to turn my belief that scientific and technological innovation can make the world a better place, into practice. In fact, this should be every Product Manager's responsibility.

A great Product Manager is also a "triple T-shaped person," with an understanding of the underlying technology, a profound grasp of human behavioural psychology, and a solid business minded appreciation of the relevant industry. This is critical as meaningful innovation is often - and increasingly so - born by weaving together advancements from multiple disciplines. Take such interdisciplinary knowledge and add a strong intuition and you have got a true creative innovator.

On the other side, the breadth of skills needed by a Product Manager to actually deliver the solution and make a substantial impact are as wide as you would expect from a good CEO - unsurprisingly it is often a path there.

What are some of the hardest challenges to overcome as a product manager?

Throughout the early stages of a product, getting user feedback is incredibly challenging. It is the time you need it most and yet it is the time it is the hardest to come by. You will have close to nothing to offer in exchange, you might not even have an MVP to show, the product is a long way from having market fit, and the company has not yet established a solid reputation. During this period, it is far too easy to get trapped in one's "amazing" vision and I have seen people fall into this trap many times. I am no different, having to constantly remind myself that it is simply against our nature to take our cherished ideas out for a beating.

© Aswin Pranam 2018
A. Pranam, *Product Management Essentials*, https://doi.org/10.1007/978-1-4842-3303-0_16

Another interesting challenge is that of culture and teams. Many companies have a great product culture and as long as you have good soft skills, slotting in is not too difficult. Startups or fresh teams on the other hand are trickier and require substantial proactive effort in building up the community, motivation, cohesion, and good collaboration. When the culture needs to be built up from scratch, a first key step is location. Often these days we work in distributed teams which makes it all the more challenging, so making sure you spend time together as a team in the beginning and then meeting up frequently and regularly with ample time for fun and bonding is critical. If, on the other hand, you have the luxury of a completely local team, nuances like seating arrangement can matter enormously - always seat your entire cross functional team together in a joint cluster - it will make building your dream team much easier.

How do you know if a product is well designed?

First, it needs to be self-explanatory. However big the pain or need you are solving is, and however good a solution you offer, unless your target audience can use it, the value it provides is zero. Of course, self-explanatory implies speed as well - even plain html can eventually be self-explanatory but applying designs and UX conventions can make it immediately intuitive.

Second and most importantly - assuming the above is trivial - the product needs to lead to the value adding result in the least amount of time. 'Value adding result' because that is ultimately the job the user is hiring the product to do - companies don't hire Google Analytics to collect and show their website data, but rather to get actionable insights on what they can do better. 'In the least amount of time,' because the faster the user achieves their goal, the more added value they gain by either being able to use the product more or by freeing up their time for other valuable activities.

Taking an airline mobile app as an example, we could improve the time component by reducing friction and automating steps, such as eliminating the tedious entering of personal and passport details for each check-in by saving and autocompleting them after the first time. Once the core value add has been optimized, we can increase the user value further by solving more pain-points including ancillary tasks. For example, the mentioned app could add the boarding pass to the phone wallet app and the flight details to the calendar automatically, right after the purchase.

What metrics do you use to track product success?

"The number of users that solve their problem with my product every time" is the success metric I have set for myself. Time spent in app, frequency of usage etc. are all proxies to this, yet can be misleading and can not be used as a general metric without taking circumstances into consideration. For example, I always buy my train tickets in the UK through an app called Trainline. The central value add they provide is for me to have a train ticket and they enable me to do that in the fastest, most self-explanatory way. Yet if they would measure time spent in app or frequency of usage, it would completely misguide them. Firstly, I only use the app briefly - which is actually desirable - to find the best train times and purchase the tickets. Secondly, the frequency of my usage is dependent on my travel schedule, something entirely out of their control. Most importantly though, I solve my previously real pain point of finding and booking trains with their app 100 percent of the time - an enormous product success.

Beyond this, making a profit or at least making enough revenue to ensure self-sustenance are critical too, depending on the type and objectives of the company.

How will the practice of building products change in the next 5–10 years?

Rather than solving a widespread problem in the same way for everyone, products will become much more individualized, both in output, features, and interaction. To continue the travel example, I would expect a flight search service (like Skyscanner) to understand what kind of trip I am trying to book from the circumstances of my specific request. When showing the results for that Friday to Sunday weekend getaway, it would know my typically acceptable departure times. It would only surface flights in that range by taking into consideration the time it will take for me to get to and from the airport, from my home or office, with my preferred mode of transport. It should do so irrespective of whether I addressed it through Siri, Alexa, or Google or whether it has to read out the results or show them on an AR interface.

Such personalisation has substantial implications for Product Managers and for how we build products. We will no longer be trying to distill the few, most common problems that represent the biggest opportunities for improvement amongst our customers. Instead, the focus will shift towards being able to best complete end-to-end idiosyncratic tasks for the largest number of users. As the individual attributes taken into consideration grow and the number of adaptive components grows with it, the complexity of the system will rapidly increase. Such 'adaptive components' could be the filter for departure time or the components for train, bus, taxi and car services to the airport as well as the various interfaces the user could interact with and switch between. The 'individual attributes' range from stable information like the home address, to learnings from historic actions, like usual flight bookings and an understanding of which meetings could likely be taken on a call whilst in transit. To enable such personalization, the trinity of Product Manager, Designer, and Lead Engineer will be joined by a new member: the learning machine. It will be the machine that will have the power to understand each individual and their nuances at scale to create the best tailored solution on the fly. Two key skills stand out for Product Managers in this new paradigm: being able to think in complex, modular systems, and an ever more important understanding and intuition for human behavior.

Tell me about a product you stopped using because it failed to meet your needs / solve a problem

As a long-time Apple user and fan, it is hard to admit that one of the biggest failures to meet a huge need for an enormous userbase is the Photos app. It is all the more devastating as the iPhone, the center of their ecosystem, is widely used to take pictures. In fact, it is said to be the most popular camera in the world and its photography features are a key driver for its purchase and upgrades. Yet, despite all of these clear reasons to invest in the downstream part of photography (enjoying the photos) as much as in the upstream (taking photos), they have failed to meet users' needs. In spite of my library of 90,000+ photos, I haven't opened my Photos app in macOS more than once in the last year and often find myself frustrated on whichever device I use it on.

First, the primary reason to take photos is to show them to someone at a later date. Yet in the Photos app on macOS, it takes about four obscure steps of removing panels and changing views until one arrives at a 'slideshow' view, and there isn't any quick way of getting back either. Contrast that to iPhotos where it was just a hit of the space bar away.

Secondly, whilst iCloud library works well, it also fails to look beyond the first step of purely storing photos and onto the actual user value of showing pictures to others at any time on any device. To enable that, the user should be able to select a number of pictures and ask Photos to store a local copy temporarily or permanently so they can edit or show them on the go and when a (good) internet connection isn't available.

Thirdly, most photos are taken during special 'happenings' where people are generally not alone. We all know the scene of everyone lining up to take the same photo when actually shared libraries are a beautifully simple way of pooling everyone's holiday pictures. Yet they are also one of the most frustrating features of iCloud Photos. Saving photos into one's own library from a shared stream will re-add existing pictures creating a host of duplicates, practically making shared libraries too tedious to be useful.

Altogether, Apple fails to serve a huge user need with how it handles photos and falls short on its own mantra of delivering outstanding user experiences that enable people to easily achieve their goals.

What is your vision for the future? Where do you think technology will take us?

I am an optimist. I like to think that we can use technology for the betterment of humankind and to overcome some of the biggest challenges facing the globe. As such I envision a world where we can once again live in much closer harmony with nature.

First, by being completely sustainable and making sustainable energy accessible to everyone. Second, by living in a manner that is closer to our 'natural' tendencies such as small, close knit communities and thirdly, by actually physically living closer within nature.

While the first point is a necessity, the latter two are not inevitable outcomes of our current trajectory. It will be very exciting to be part of shifting the world away from urbanisation towards more rural living, thereby decreasing our environmental impact, forming smaller, closer communities, giving people more living space and allowing us to find joys in nature. This will of course require a host of new technologies, from AR and VR to autonomous flying vehicles or hyperloops that can rapidly take people into urban zones from distant places every once in a while, for cultural, intellectual, work, and social activities.

PART IV

Business & Management Foundations

CHAPTER 17

■ ■ ■

Playing the part

"Does it better" will always beat "did it first."

—Aaron Levie

All the technical and design skill in the world won't save you as a product manager if you're lacking the number one skill required to succeed in the role: leadership. If you enter a team, establish yourself in your new role, and nominate yourself as the go-to resource for managing the development of a new product, you NEED to understand the "soft skills" that come into play when managing conflicting sets of interests.

Strip away the titles, meetings, and day-to-day tasks, and you're left with a group of regular human beings who are coordinating their time on this earth around a common goal. Engineer A may be in the middle of selling his house, Designer B may have been passed up on a promotion twice, and Marketer C may be going through a divorce. Although all of this could seem like personal issues that should be abstracted away from a person's ability to perform at work, they matter.

If you've done research around hiring at enterprises, you'll see a bit of literature around the "layover test." This states that if you have two candidates who meet a baseline level of skill required for a position, you should choose the one you'd want to grab a drink or coffee with during an airport layover from destination A to B. As simple as it sounds, people like being around people they like. More importantly, they want to work with people who see them as an individual instead of a means to an end.

In this section, we'll cover ways you can inspire confidence with the engineering team, talk to leadership without their eyes glazing over, and handle yourself in a way that people can get behind.

© Aswin Pranam 2018

A. Pranam, *Product Management Essentials*, https://doi.org/10.1007/978-1-4842-3303-0_17

Leading without authority

The organizational chart of today's typical tech enterprise starts with a CEO at the top of the hierarchy, followed by a line of executives directly underneath, split by business function. The product manager is restricted to the "product ladder," and only has purview over the PMs that fall directly below their management tier. This presents a set of unique advantages (training from leaders who understand the function, cross-collaboration with other PMs, etc.) but it can also confuse first time PMs.

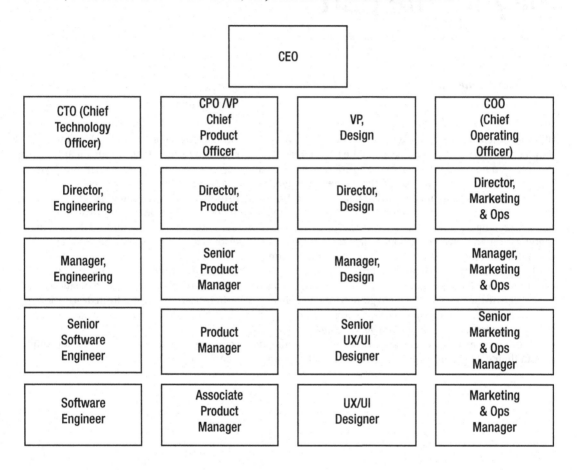

If you don't have explicit authority over the team of engineers and designers, how do you convince them to follow your recommendations?

This is where the intangible skill of leadership comes in. To lead without direct authority as a PM, you have to expand your horizons and tap into the incentives of each person you're trying to influence. Challenges come with developing relationships within every node in this interconnected political network, but following a set of tips can go a long way.

Tips to lead effectively

- <u>Listen</u>: A good leader knows when to keep their ears open and their mouths shut. Being attentive and responsive tells people that you care about what they have to say.

- <u>Practice Empathy</u>: Understanding one another fosters trust, and realizing that human beings don't exist to check off tasks at work goes a long way. If someone is going through a rough patch or dealing with difficult circumstances, step back, put yourself in their shoes, and act based on the holistic view of the situation.

- <u>Establish credibility</u>: Understand the user, market, product, and problem space. Even if you lack the technical or design chops, a firm understanding of the industry landscape is enough to add value.

- <u>Discard hierarchy</u>: Don't pull rank to push a point forward. Use data and rational insights to break down ideas that aren't feasible instead of brute forcing your viewpoint on the team.

- <u>Avoid criticism</u>: Follow a "yes, and..." approach by extending thoughts previously suggested by team members and flexing them to reflect your ideas. Directly criticizing and shutting down team members disrupts the creative flow and adds tension to team dynamics.

- <u>Set a positive example</u>: Carry yourself with a sense of purpose, establish a high moral and ethical bar, and praise team members and peers who exceed expectations.

- <u>Rally around a vision and clear set of goals</u>: Believe in the end goal so passionately that the team has no choice but to align themselves with you.

- <u>Establish strong views, but keep them loosely held</u>: Keep a firm position at all times in regard to approved decisions, but be willing to change at a moment's notice if new information that counters the original hypothesis emerges.

Learn to communicate ideas

We all know the saying: "communication is key." Key to a good relationship, personal satisfaction, and life success. In product management, the same sentiment still holds true. People want to know what is going on with a project, and knowing the "right" way to communicate to an audience can set the stage for you to shine as a product manager.

When it comes to matters of relaying information and translating complex thoughts through speech, the PM's approach will change based on which of three stakeholders they're interacting with: team members, upper management, and users.

Communication: Upper Management

Managers, executives, and board members have no interest in a verbal essay of the product development gameplan; they only want to know that things are on track and on budget. When communicating upstream, keep in mind that they don't have visibility into the day-to-day, so the PM's goal is to select the major themes of the past week / month / year and find a medium to communicate this in the most effective way. A poor sense of communication can cast a black mark on a PM and prevent them from being at the table for important conversations, so practice speaking to leadership and ask for feedback after the session for the sake of continuous improvement.

Best practices

- <u>Keep it concise:</u> Executives and senior managers are busy people. Cover the major points, and leave enough room for clarifying questions. Anticipate the value they're looking to extract from the conversation, and tailor your presentation to fit this objective.

- <u>Active communication:</u> Send emails, pings, or Slack messages to constantly engage members of leadership when appropriate. If you fall off their radar, it can be hard to build the relationship later down the line.

- <u>Avoid general answers:</u> For one-on-ones with line managers or directors, don't answer with "everything is fine" or "I'm fine" every time. Don't be afraid to bring points of concern to their attention, and never hold back when things are falling apart (or when things are successful!).

- <u>Focus on business value:</u> Saying "feature X, Y, and Z have been implemented" isn't useful to an individual in leadership. Instead, hone in on why it's important for pushing the business forward and adding value. For example, "Feature X will allow us to track the number of users who convert based on the ads we're deploying, allowing us to allocate marketing spend more effectively" is a solid way to signal that the feature has been marked done, and the resulting value-adding effect of deploying it to the customer.

Communication: Users

Press releases, help center documentation, newsletters, and media announcements are all examples of ways the company will need to communicate offerings to the customer. The product manager will directly or indirectly touch each form of user communication, and frame the correct tone and language to connect with the target audience. A game manufacturer will want to use engaging, explosive language to promote a new first-person shooter, whereas a B2B enterprise startup needs to invoke a sense of professionalism and credibility with their communication strategy.

Best practices

- <u>Understand the audience:</u> Align yourself with the user's point of view. Use language that is familiar and easy to comprehend.

- <u>Simplify:</u> Don't overcomplicate for the sake of sounding professional (except in rare cases). Stick to tried and true methods, but never speak down to the user or insult their intelligence.

- <u>Personalize the message:</u> Users don't want to feel like they are one of a million others in a calculated batch. Targeted outreach with a personal touch can go a long way to leaving a lasting, positive impression.

- <u>Study indirect channels of feedback:</u> Internet forums, comments, and other ancillary channels of user engagement are a gold mine for tapping into the voice of the user and capturing their raw, unfiltered response to the product or service.

Communication: Team Members

Open. Honest. Transparent. When delivering news to the team and communicating progress, it's imperative that everyone is evenly filled in. Team members should not feel out of the loop, or feel like they need to set up meetings with the product manager just to stay updated on what's going on. To kickstart a PM's communication model, the following set of channels in the figure below can be leveraged to make sure knowledge distribution is widespread and nobody is left in the dark.

Effective Communication	
Weekly / Bi-Weekly Updates	• Short, digestible update (PowerPoint / Google Slides) • Features completed this week / milestones achieved • Planned work for next week / anticipated risks or roadblocks
Presentations	• Clear, vocal communication to board or upper management • Tells a story and glosses over details unless necessary • Know your audience / anticipate their questions
Daily Comms	• Questions, concerns, and general team communication • Bite-sized threads that may / may not lead to larger meetings • Slack, Microsoft Teams -- software tool options
Vision / Roadmap	• Central portal with features/bugs, roadmap, and progress • Lists ideas, designs, and documentation from development • JIRA, Pivotal Tracker, ProdPad -- software tool options
Mailing Lists	• Subset of larger team focused only on product / tech • Miscelleanous discussions and thought bubbles • Create clear aliases (e.g. product@teamname.com)

Best practices

- Treat the inner circle like family: Whatever the PM knows, the team knows. Be liberal about disseminating information, and the team's trust will be won sooner than later (or never).

- Create an open atmosphere: Debate, discuss, and encourage discourse in a safe, collaborative space.

- <u>Don't play the blame game:</u> Mistakes and wrong calls are a given in the development workstream, and pointing out individual slip ups isn't productive. Focus on the lessons learned, and don't dwell on failure by singling out members who made an incorrect decision.

- <u>Establish a lasting personal relationship:</u> Eat lunch, go bowling, or grab a beer with team members. It's much, much harder to work with people you only know on a superficial level.

The Art of Negotiation

I recently went to a car dealership to purchase a new vehicle. A mix of excitement and nervousness rushing through my body on this monumental day, I stepped inside the building with an idea of the estimated trade-in value I hoped to receive for my current vehicle. After viewing the car I wanted, I sat down at the negotiation table and shot across my trade-in offer. The dealer representative paused, said "I'll speak to my manager" and went upstairs, and came down a few minutes later. He agreed to my dollar amount without countering. Ecstatic and surprised, I happily continued with the process and purchased my new vehicle.

In retrospect, it's clear to me now that I lost the negotiation.

Negotiations are never easy. If the other side folds immediately, it's because you didn't ask for enough or they have a gameplan in place to mitigate the expected loss on their end. The same is true with software and product development. A product manager will often be in the business of making tradeoffs and convincing people to do things they aren't necessarily thrilled about. To soften the headache of negotiation, the PM can use a set of tried and true conventions to sway the verbal tug-of-war in their favor.

<u>Mirroring:</u> Mimic the movements of the other person, repeat their ideas back to them before framing your own opinion, and match their mood and cadence.

<u>Listening to your inner EQ:</u> Observe visual cues (e.g., is the person in a hurry? Are they constantly checking their watch?), pick up on microexpressions, and get a sense of their immediate reaction to statements you make. If the conversation is not progressing in a positive direction, be able to adapt on the fly to avoid damaging the negotiation.

<u>Avoid haste decision-making:</u> Do not commit (or overcommit) to anything based on just one discussion. Let the points stand, and give everyone time to sleep on it. Often times, if the other party is willing to immediately accept a path that leaves them with the short end of the deal, that should be a red flag signaling to you that time is needed to think through all possible exit scenarios.

<u>Lose the battle to win the war:</u> Aggressively pursuing a win in each debate will land you in hot water and mark you with a toxic reputation. Find strategic moments to give in and accept a less favorable outcome to position yourself for a pivotal win in a future negotiation.

<u>Chase cooperative agreement:</u> Win-win scenarios do exist. If option A and B are being negotiated, but a third option C naturally emerges which is beneficial for both parties without as much compromise from either end, then it should float to the top of the list of acceptable outcomes.

Personal Development

In the chase to develop timeless products, paying close attention to personal growth is imperative to climbing the ranks and adding more responsibility to your plate as your career grows. The quickest way to maximize learning potential and level up fast is to use the resources directly around you.

<u>Mentorship:</u> Seek out 2–3 senior managers / executives within the organization who can guide your career. Studying their path and understanding their trials and tribulations effectively prevents you from hitting the roadblocks that they've bumped into in the past.

Community building: Use internal tools and shared community resources to create a culture that nurtures and develops product talent within the company. Share best practices, artifacts, and tips to help each other reach a state of collective product excellence.

Source feedback: Positive feedback is great for self-confidence, but negative feedback is where the gold lies. Ask teammates and colleagues to provide detailed feedback from both ends without restraint, and put together a plan to flip your weaknesses into strengths.

N+1 performance: A product manager level 1 should strive to perform at a PM level 2 standard, and a PM level 2 should constantly work at a PM level 3 baseline, and so on. Never settle on performing at par with the current state job expectations; aim higher and set a trajectory that exceeds the bar.

Conclusion

The product manager role is tough and comes with stress, high expectations, and moments of self-doubt. Coordinating the balance between a plethora of teams and managing the sky-high expectations of leadership is no small task, but harnessing the knowledge and expertise of your engineering team, fellow PMs, and mentors can smooth out the rough edges and pump up the probability of success. Rely on the team, believe in your own abilities, and trust the process.

■ ■ ■

CHAPTER 18

Product Strategy

"Incremental innovation is basically just adjusting for inflation"

—@BoredElonMusk twitter account

Innovation is a term that penetrated the business and technology lexicon ages ago and still billed as the only way to stay relevant in the information age. New product entering the market? Innovative. Software update? Innovative. Slight refresh of a couple UI components? Innovative. When everything is labeled as being innovative, nothing really is.

Businesses forget that as they're managing and developing in-house innovation hubs, other companies are doing the same. Absolute progress continues to move forward, but relative positioning stays exactly the same. The tech industry's own version of the Red Queen's race.

To compete in today's markets, we need to chase disruptive innovation. The goal is to build products that become so deeply entrenched in our psyche and daily ability to function that we couldn't have imagined life before without it. To do this, we need a strategy. In this chapter, we'll examine ways to put together product documents, develop strategic plans, and touch on other considerations a product manager needs to be aware of in the scope of their project.

Forecasting the unknown

Legendary hockey player Wayne Gretzky was once quoted as saying "I skate to where the puck is going, not where it has been." To paraphrase into a tech-relevant phrase, product managers need to "build for the future, not the present." Software projects can range from six months at the low end all the way to 5+ years depending on the scope, complexity, and commitment.

With this in mind, how does the product manager forecast into the unknown and know where a user's priorities will be years down the line?

The key is to pay attention to industry trends and integrate the cutting edge into aspects of the product being built. Today, machine learning, blockchain, and IoT are red hot, but the seasoned PM will know what is a fad destined to phase out in the near term and what can change the way products are developed five to ten years from now. Pay attention to the direction industry players are moving in, and pick and choose technologies that offer distinct advantages. Also, just because something hasn't been done doesn't mean it isn't theoretically possible. Aim high and act ambitiously. The tech world is running out of room for more "Me-Too" products.

© Aswin Pranam 2018
A. Pranam, *Product Management Essentials*, https://doi.org/10.1007/978-1-4842-3303-0_18

Budgeting & Estimation

When the CEO is putting together a budget proposal for the year, or new product development is scheduled to kick off, the recurring question that comes up is "how much do we need for product and engineering?"

For a new PM, it can be daunting and overwhelming to come up with a solid figure.

When assigning dollar figures to a proposal, keep in mind the following expenses:

- Labor (salaries)
- Software licenses (task management tools, source control, project management platforms, etc.)
- Hosting (cloud and bare metal servers)
- Equipment (computers and hardware)
- Open-source technologies
- Off-the-shelf technologies
- Third-party development
- Miscellaneous (travel, food, hotels)
- Training
- Development operations (penetration testing, moving from development to production, etc.)

Once an initial estimate is calculated, run it by the engineering managers, other product managers, and anyone else who has experience in this space. Everyone will have opinions, but if you reach a state where the estimates are all within an acceptable range, then you have your rough number.

■ **Note**   The number one rule to budgeting and estimation is to **add a buffer.** If the final figure is $1.2 million, add an additional 25% on top to offset unforeseen costs that can and will arise. Asking for more and having funds left over is always preferred to running out of money and stalling development until more budget is allocated.

Vendor management

Dealing with vendors can either be a headache or pleasure depending on who, what, and how much. At some point in your product career, you'll have to either rely on a full-time dedicated vendor team to understand your creative vision, or supplement an internal workforce with outside talent to pick up tasks that the main team doesn't have the time to execute. When sourcing a third-party vendor, you will come across tons of development shops (domestic and international) that want to bid for your budget. Finding a trusted vendor and establishing a long-term relationship is what every product manager hopes for, but in any case, it's wise to remember a handful of guidelines when hiring contractors.

- Double check the SOW (Statement of Work): The SOW details what needs to be delivered, as well as the expenses associated with final handoff. Run the SOW by the legal team and ensure that your organization is protected in the event of unsuccessful completion. The SOW is the trusted handshake between two parties, so make sure everything about the project is included in this document.

- <u>Fixed vs. variable cost:</u> Some projects will be a fixed fee, others will vary based on time committed. Be sure not to assume that a variable price contract can't go significantly above the agreed upon rate (hint: it can).

- <u>Agile vs. waterfall:</u> If the development team is using agile methodologies for software development, it can be tough to set an end date to the project. Don't make recommendations to management that tie the team to a fixed month and day. Add buffer in the timeline and keep estimates to a 2–3 month window to be safe.

- <u>Controlling scope:</u> The SOW doesn't list every feature and design requirement, so it's essential to sit down with the vendor and use the PRD as a blueprint. Understand that scope will change throughout the project, and features can be added / dropped based on velocity and other considerations.

Studying the competition

Before starting a development cycle, the research phase will contain a competitive assessment stage. Spending time building a product only to find out later than a competitor with majority market share already exists is a bad way to go back to square one. To run a proper competitive assessment, tap into expert networks, pay research firms to pull information on market leaders in the space you're targeting, and become a domain expert so you can spot the fakes from the real threats. A framework for modeling relationships in a delicate, competitive ecosystem that is widely referenced is **Porter's 5 forces**. The concept describes the forces that make an industry competitive or attractive based on the power position of incumbents. Using the five areas of focus and tailoring it to existing players can give a high-level view of opportunities and entry points, as shown in Figure 18-1.

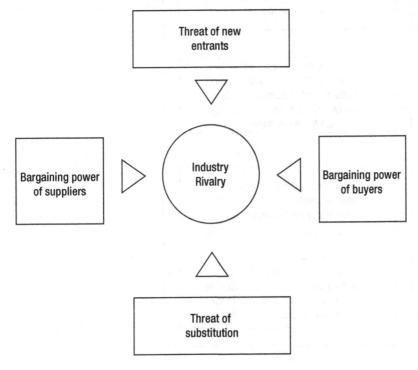

Figure 18-1. *A high-level view of opportunities and entry points*

Marketing 101

Let's look at the basics of marketing.

The 4 Ps

A product manager is not a marketer, but they interface enough with the marketing manager and team that terms and ideas will be picked up along the way. One ubiquitous tool for understanding product differentiators and the components of the overall marketing mix are the 4 Ps. The Ps are product, price, promotion, and place (see Figure 18-2). To use this model properly, consider drafting questions around each P and asking if your product has a satisfying answer. For example:

- Is the product priced competitively among the competition?

- Is the product readily available to purchase in areas with a concentration of target users?

- What is the proper channel to promote the product?

- What is the core differentiator of the product we are releasing?

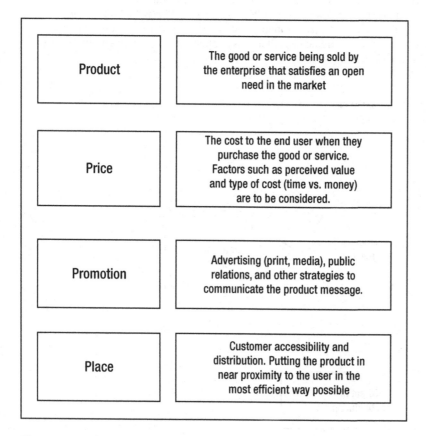

Figure 18-2. The 4 Ps

MARKETING: THROUGH THE LENS

A concept that many people forget about is the promotion of their product. You can have an excellent product, but if you don't put any marketing horsepower behind it, the results may vary. In 2014, I was working on a news aggregator app. During its initial launch, it was well received by users and downloads grew organically through word of mouth recommendations. However, it was not prioritized internally when it came to distribution of marketing spend. The company focused on promoting bigger bets, and this lead to the news app falling out of the trending apps and ultimately being sunsetted. A small percentage of products are so good that they essentially sell themselves, but if a user isn't aware your product exists, they'll have no option but to go with a close competitor.

On the flip side, I've also seen examples of marketing being leveraged correctly to spark off user engagement at exponential rates. One of the products I've worked on in the fantasy sports and statistics domain managed to increase the user base in the order of millions of users per month by adding more money to the marketing budget. The effort was massive, and required all hands on deck, but the payoff was well worth it. Users were happy to use the product, and revenues justified the marketing bill. Without a marketing plan, the product's potential would have remained under the surface for a long, long time.

At the heart of it all, the product has to be good; there's not enough marketing budget in the world that can substitute a product that solves a real issue. But, a product that solves a problem can get lost in the shuffle if it isn't promoted properly. Hundreds (if not thousands) of apps, websites, and other software products are released daily, and you need a way to stand out in a sea of competition. Marketing can do this, and the uptick in user growth that comes with a dedicated marketing effort can be the X-factor for an impressive product launch.

Sulman Haque, Sr. Business Planning Analyst at Oath (formerly known as Yahoo)

Go-to-market strategy

A go-to-market strategy is the structured plan describing of all the marketing and promotional legwork required to reach customers and distribute the product to the wider audience. The go-to-market includes:

- The core value proposition

- Identification of target demographic

- Plans to reach the intended audience

- Factors of differentiation from industry leaders / competitors

- An overview of the marketing mix

- Brand positioning

- Establishing channels for promotion and awareness building

An overarching template for a go-to-market strategy doesn't exist since it is tailored to the industry and company, but the development of this plan is advised because it mitigates reputational risk, enhances brand awareness, and shrinks the actual time to market for new product development. The marketing landscape is vast, and one company's favored approach won't work for another. For a product manager, your job is to sit in the room and align on the way the product is positioned to the customers and provide input on the strategic goals. In the end, the go-to-market will be aligned with the company's product strategy and the two will go hand-in-hand to ensure a successful launch.

Product Requirements Document (PRD)

Writing a comprehensive, detailed PRD is a task that separates the good PMs from the high performers. The product requirements document is a manifest of all the features, requirements, and considerations identified before kicking off formal development. It communicates what a product should do, and the assumptions made prior to deeper analysis performed at later stages.

A proper PRD contains the following pieces of information:

- Header / Authorship: Title and names of all the authors (usually the product manager with contributors)

- Project Objectives / Goals: Purpose of the project, and the goals needed to be met once development is over.

- Scope: Describes the product, and specifically mentions out-of-scope requirements left for another version.

- High-Level Description: Short description of background / context, product information, and industry landscape.

- Stakeholders: All of the non-team members with a vested interest in project execution and success.

- Project Team: Lists titles, roles, and responsibilities of each member in the product development team.

- Product Overview: A longer, detailed view of the product discussing the key outcomes and features of this release.

- Functional Requirements: Requirements that describe what the product should do (e.g., the system sends an automatic email confirmation when a user is added)

- Non-functional Requirements: Requirements that describe how the product behaves (e.g., the product should have an uptime of 99.99%).

- Proposed Tech Stack: Runs through the software stack and the rationale behind chosen technologies.

- Timelines / Milestones: Estimated time window to completion along with pivotal milestones.

- Assumptions: Describes conditions which are thought to be true upon start of development.

- Risks / Constraints: Any and all risks that can throw the scope, budget, or timeline out of whack with mitigation plans for each. Also, constraints that limit development are included in this section.

- Future Development: Plans for the next version of the product and deferred feature sets.

- Open Questions: Unanswered queries that need to be clarified or closed out.

Product Roadmap

The roadmap is the living, breathing representation of the company's product strategy. It communicates the now, next, and future development plans, and tracks the state of live products and their development paths. A roadmap can be represented as a thorough document, or mapped in a tool like ProdPad or Aha!

Here are the product roadmap goals:

- Measure progress against KPIs and trackable metrics

- Provide view on every product in the portfolio in one centralized place

- Secure buy-in from leadership and related stakeholders

- Tie product success to business goals

- Provide visibility for the internal teams to understand where the products are headed

- Rally around a unifying mission statement, and use this to direct decision-making

Use the roadmap to tell a story (an example is in Figure 18-3). Make it compelling and provide rationale for the set timelines. Granularity of information is based on personal preference, but enough detail to answer the pressing questions that come to mind for team members and leadership is enough to keep it live and active.

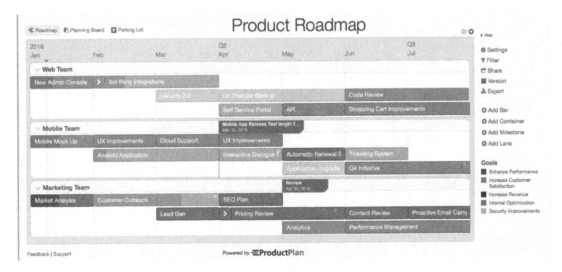

Figure 18-3. Example Product Roadmap from ProductPlan

Conclusion

The specific techniques you develop early in your product career will become muscle memory after a couple of product deployments. Build good habits early, become comfortable with frequent documentation, and treat the artifacts you create as an extension of your verbally communicated vision. An organized PM with a clear strategy comforts the team and keeps leadership happy. And remember: there is enough randomness to the product role that at times, nobody knows what they're doing. Fall back on what you know to be true, and stick to the plan :)

■ ■ ■

CHAPTER 19

Industry Spotlight: Q&A with Amelia Crook

Amelia started her digital career as a content editor but soon found herself drawn to user experience and business dynamics so transitioned to product management. She is a performance-driven and analytical product manager with experience building successful products for leading online companies around the world including Amazon, Lonely Planet, Martha Stewart, and some of Australia's most successful startups. She values and enjoys a collaborative approach to building products. She is skilled at taking complex problems, breaking them down and setting a clear vision and roadmap to success.

What does the term "product manager" mean to you?

Leading a team of different disciplines and setting a vision for them to work together to build something that provides value to users and the business.

What's the best piece of advice you have for new product managers?

Listen and learn from your customers, from your development and design colleagues, and from other people in the business. Your job is not to know everything, but you do need to have a good understanding of all parts of the business to be an effective product manager.

What misconception do people generally have about the product manager role?

I think the "CEO of the product" description of product management can lead people to believe that the role is fully autonomous and that they will get to make all the decisions. This isn't the case.

Effective product managers collaborate, communicate, and influence. They align teams behind a shared vision and strategy and enable that team to make great decisions that are aligned to the goals of the business.

© Aswin Pranam 2018
A. Pranam, *Product Management Essentials*, https://doi.org/10.1007/978-1-4842-3303-0_19

What's your favorite interview question for a product manager?

I like to ask about decisions that turned out to be the wrong ones and what they learned from that experience. The ability to be lean and agile in your thinking and reflect and learn from mistakes is more important than being right all of the time.

Describe your process for prioritizing requirements

Prioritization is an exercise in understanding what features and requirements are going to have the most impact in terms of meeting your goal.

That implies that the goal needs to be very clear and understood by everyone; you can't prioritize without a clear goal.

Prioritizing based on that goal and doing it transparently with your team is the most effective way of avoiding confusion and gaining a shared understanding of what's important and why. This also means that the micro decisions team members are making in the code or in the design are more likely to stay aligned as well.

What's the best way to validate an idea with users before moving forward with development?

I wholly subscribe to Marty Cagan's teaching around addressing four key risks in discovery: value, usability, feasibility, and business.

Every project will require a different toolset to explore these risks, but a) understanding the numbers and what success looks like b) talking to users c) exploring the technical implications and d) talking to key business partners like lawyers and customer service is always key.

■ ■ ■

CHAPTER 20

Crossing the finish line

Home stretch. At this stage of the game, you've absorbed pages and pages of information that will contribute to your development as a product manager. In this final chapter, I'll walk through miscellaneous nuggets of knowledge that didn't logically fit into the previous chapters, followed by a Q&A that answers any lingering questions that weren't covered by the industry spotlights. In essence, I want to attempt to tie any remaining loose ends and finish strong. If you still have thoughts, concerns, or questions, I'll happily make my email available (contact@aswinpranam.com) to field leftover queries.

Abandon Fear

Fear is a useless emotion in product management. The analysis, decision-making, and research conducted before the product steps into development should give the PM enough confidence to jump into the unknown without being held back by fear or doubt. If the team senses that the PM is unsure about the product path, it can cause a domino effect that can hurt morale and team motivation. If the road chosen returns nothing, go back and pick a new path.

Think like Spock, lead like Kirk

For those of you who aren't Trekkies (myself included), Captain Kirk and Spock are both characters from the popular Star Trek franchise. Kirk, a capable, charismatic leader who instills confidence in his subordinates and manages the team, is complemented by Spock, a calculated, analytical thinker who has perfected the art of emotional stability and rational thinking. In a work environment, you're expected to be both the brain and the heart, which can be a tricky thing to master.

A PM representation of Kirk will speak up at meetings, sit at the head of the table (both literally and figuratively), defend his or her team members (engineers / designers / etc.), and make the tough calls when nobody else can. At the same time, the PM will have to understand the data (models, research, studies, etc.), advise the engineering team on pros & cons if relevant, and keep a cool head if tensions flare.

All in all, keep your cool. People will test you, things will go haywire, and egos will emerge in the conference room. Be tactical in your thinking and never react based off of emotion alone.

© Aswin Pranam 2018
A. Pranam, *Product Management Essentials*, https://doi.org/10.1007/978-1-4842-3303-0_20

Don't ask permission, just ask forgiveness

Corporate bureaucracy and red tape can hinder your ability to innovate. On one hand, rules are put in place to protect you and the company. Sending unencrypted emails containing sensitive information to vendors and skirting the process designed to secure data to save time is a bad idea. But, there are grey areas where calls need to be made, and you don't have time to pull together every single point of approval. Exercise good judgement, but bend the rules where necessary.

Don't always rely on "best practices"

Best practices were put in place based on observations from history. If 100 projects all used one method and 95 percent of them succeeded, the process is documented and branded as a best practice for all teams to follow. Often times, there are "better practices" waiting to be discovered. In essence, a best practice is just a baseline; it's what everyone else is doing. As the timescale changes from year to year, the same recommendations won't work. Find new ways to improve on the status quo, and refresh the thinking each year so you're not relying on outdated models of thought.

Embrace exponential thinking

Human beings are bad exponential thinkers and predictors. If we're asked to predict the next 20, 50, or 100 years of technological development, we'd be terribly inaccurate once the time has come and passed. This handicap restricts us from seeing things how they will be instead of focused just on how they are. The next century will be defined by those that can make calculated bets on emerging technologies that will outlast the hype. Train yourself to accept and anticipate radical change, and find a way to put yourself at the bleeding edge so your job isn't on the chopping block as a direct result of exponential tech growth.

Dealing with failure

Failure is not an end state; it's a minor road bump along the path to success. I've never known a product manager who had a perfect record when it came to product deployments, so don't set unreasonable expectations for yourself. If a launch or decision ends up producing results you're unhappy with, go back to the drawing board and start over. Being frustrated in the aftermath of a bad call isn't productive, but using the learnings to influence the next iteration may lead to a home run the second time around.

Never underestimate the power of luck

Success is not 100 percent attributed to skill and hard work. Luck can be the factor that makes or breaks a product, and doing everything you can to maximize the amount of luck that falls on your side is a wise decision. For example, if a cybersecurity startup is entering the market, a spring of hacks that pop up at once can be a golden opportunity to reach out to the companies affected and negotiate a contract to provide products or services. Capitalize on acts of God or dumb luck moments, because you will need a lucky break every once in a while to provide relief and dissolve pressure from the team.

10 Q's

How do I hire a product manager?

Carefully. Pulling people from related roles like technical program manager or finding strategic thinkers from areas like consulting can be the best bet if your organization hasn't formalized internal requirements for a product role. Since the role is still relatively new, there is no prescribed way to hire strong PMs. Talk to leaders in the community, source their advice, and above all, tease out critical thinking ability in the list of candidates you interview.

What if the organization I join doesn't understand the product role?

A common issue. Companies, especially non-tech firms, will either convert a "project manager" into a product manager to capitalize on the buzz surrounding the role, or will hire a product manager and stick them with marketing and customer service responsibilities without any direct pull on engineering or the product being built. If you're outside of the organization, ask questions during the interview and be sure the role involves touching the core product. If you're inside the organization, approach the top-line management leader and set time on the calendar to discuss expectations for a PM role and provide your two cents. Often times, leadership is willing to make changes because they're under the assumption that nothing is wrong. Be a voice for product, and build a product culture that you'd be proud of, piece by piece.

What if I have a limited budget for product development and engineering?

A tight budget is not necessarily a bad thing if you're tasked with producing an MVP. The scope for an MVP is limited, and non-critical features can be stripped away since it will be used as a proof-of-concept to test the market. However, if you're building a V2 and beyond product, it can be difficult to push ahead without adequate resources. Going with cheaper development is an option, but it can come with a quality tradeoff. The best move forward is to communicate the final deliverable with $ budget to leadership so they are well aware of what is realistic, and show them a mock or improved version of the product that can be built with $$$ budget. It could be a useful tactic to convince them to allocate more funds, or it can just set expectations accordingly if you deliver a subpar product with the resources you were given.

What if I'm not respected?

Find a way to earn it. People are motivated by incentives, and those who don't respect you feel that way because of something you did or didn't do, so think of ways you can attract others by helping them help themselves. Pull people into a meeting, ask them for advice, or send them documents for review. Small moves that make peers feel included and showing them that their opinions are valued can go a long way.

What can I start doing today to flex my product management muscles?

Create a product in your free time. Put together a business plan, go-to-market strategy, mock PRD, mock roadmap, and use Balsamiq or Sketch to put together wireframes. If you have the resources, find engineers who can build it and manage the development journey. Or go online and donate your product management skills for free to build experience and a portfolio of pro-bono projects. The best way of learning is doing, so get involved.

Is an MBA required to be a product manager?

No. An MBA can help solidify the business fundamentals, but it can't immediately make you product-ready. Utilizing 2 years on a full-time program can be valuable to some, but others will be better off in the workforce for two years. If you can work full-time and get a part-time MBA, even better.

What are the growth opportunities for a product manager?

There is no glass ceiling for a product manager. Sundar Pichai (Google) and Marissa Mayer (Yahoo) are examples of product managers turned CEOs, so there's no limit to how high you can go. Find an organization that has a clear promotion path, be impactful, and the rest will take care of itself.

Join a startup as PM #1 or an established company as PM #1000?

This is a tough one, and depends entirely on the person making the decision. I've boiled down a handful of pros and cons to each below.

Startup PM #1

–   Control over the entire product portfolio; single point of responsibility for strategy

–   Lower base salary, but high equity stake

–   Wider scope of responsibilities beyond product due to size of company (marketing, customer service, picking up takeout, etc.)

–   Limited resources and funds

Established company PM #1000

–   Control over a single product, but can be a billion-dollar service line or market opportunity

–   Higher base salary, lower equity stake in the form of restricted stock units (if any)

–   Narrow scope of responsibility; focus on just one vertical

–   Well resourced / fewer budget constraints

Is it detrimental to my career to join a product team at a non-tech company?

Absolutely not. Every company will have a technology function, and non-tech companies are ripe for disruption. If taxi companies embraced innovation a long time ago, Uber would never have been launched and yellow cabs would have a stronghold on the transportation market.

I've heard PMs work 80-100 hour weeks. How do I avoid this?

False. Hours of work does not equal productivity. Every additional hour you dedicate beyond a reasonable threshold has diminishing returns, and positions you for burnout. A healthy 40-60 hour work week is achievable, and it's all about keeping track of priorities. Finish the urgent tasks first, say no to people to avoid over promising, and treat your mental and physical health with the same level of care as your career.

Additional Resources

A collection of learning outlets and tools to keep your product knowledge fresh and relevant.
Product bootcamps

- Specialized learning centers are popping up all across the country, and a couple are centered around developing product talent in 8-10 weeks. The effectiveness of the programs are yet to be vetted, but it's worth researching if you are in a completely different industry looking to transition.

MOOCs

- Massive Open Online Courses (MOOCs) allow students from all over the world to tune in and sharpen their technical skillset. A couple of solid companies (Udacity, Coursera) have courses taught from top professors around UX, software engineering, and data analysis.

Must Reads

- Crossing the chasm

- Zero to One

- Lean Startup

- Hooked

- Design of everyday things

- The imposter's handbook

- The personal MBA

A call to action

On February 19, 2017, Susan Fowler dropped a bombshell on the tech industry that reverberated all throughout Silicon Valley. A skilled female engineer at Uber, Susan opened Pandora's box when she revealed counts of discrimination, sexual harassment, and unfair treatment within the org hierarchy of Uber. In the months following, an unsettling number of women came forward, both internally and externally to speak of their experiences being inappropriately propositioned, objectified, and intimidated.

To all the current and future product managers who read this, we can and need to do better. An ideal PM is responsible in part for dictating culture, upholding values, and being an ethically sound model citizen, inside and outside the walls of a tech enterprise.

If you witness harassment, unfair treatment, or discrimination, don't shy away or turn a blind eye to it. Speak up. Attack it head on, and stand your ground. To build the future of technology, we need to do it together, and the current diversity rates across the industry are abysmal.

Let's pledge to stand up for our peers and colleagues, and take the small but vital steps to eradicate this vein of dangerous thinking from the industry permanently.

Commencement

Whew, you've made it through. Throughout this 150+ page journey, we've covered process, strategy, design, development, and lessons from top-tier professionals along the way. We haven't covered everything, and there are certainly knowledge gaps that come with packing so much into a slim cookbook, but I hope you've understood the potential of the product manager role.

First off, I want to say thank you to the readers. In this brief exchange of time, money, and mental brainpower from your side, my wish is that you've come to one of three conclusions:

Wow, product is exciting. I need to become a PM and enter this role ASAP!

Product is dull. I'll stick to what I'm doing now, thanks. Plus, this manual was garbage, sorry.

I'm still undecided, but I learned skills along the way that will serve me well irrespective of what I end up doing.

Even if just one person is inspired to enter the tech industry (or product specifically), I've done my job and will happily sleep at night.

Second, it is my firm belief that every company will become a technology company in the next 15-20 years, if not sooner. Software is eating the world, and you may be surprised at how fast development is accelerating. Machines are defeating human beings at skilled tasks (AlphaGo), jobs are being replaced rapidly (self-driving cars/trucks), and companies are finding ways to stay ahead of the curve by hiring the best engineers, product managers, and tech talent with exorbitant compensation packages. I recently shared a flight with a C-suite executive of a bicycle manufacturer who told me their competitive advantage in the past year and beyond will be software engineering. A bicycle company. Wild.

Lastly, keep learning. The industry will move forward without you, whether you like it or not. People often overestimate the amount of time it takes to learn a new skill or understand a new technology. Spending just 15-30 minutes a day to read through Hacker News, skim articles on TechCrunch, or stepping through tutorials online can have a profound effect on your career. I recently sat down with a colleague who majored in computer science five years ago, but feels out of touch with recent developments and frameworks in the web space. If he's falling behind, so are you if you don't dedicate yourself. Read blogs, attend meetups, speak to subject matter experts. Never let the fire or passion die, and seek out new reservoirs of inspiration if you feel burned out.

And with that, I'll wrap up. Good luck, and I can't wait to see the transformative products that the next generation of product managers put in the hands of consumers.

Until next time.

"Coding is a beautiful thing…If there is a God, he definitely codes. There are fail-safes in the world. That's code. I don't want young black kids to aspire to be rappers or ballers. Even lawyers and doctors— those are service positions. I want them to be coders. They can make their own worlds then. They don't need anybody else. I love hearing those kids' ideas, all these kids on the Internet. The excitement of making something, that's the spark of God." - Donald Glover (Childish Gambino) / Interview with Complex.com

■ ■ ■

CHAPTER 21

Industry Spotlight: Q&A with Romy Macasieb

Romy Macasieb is the VP of Product Management at Walker & Company Brands, where he leads the digital Product and Creative teams. Prior to Walker & Company, Romy was the Head of Product for a startup called ThisLife - a service that pulled all the photos and videos you had stored across social networks and devices, and organized them all in one place. ThisLife was later acquired by Shutterfly, where Romy built new experiences for iOS, Android, and Kindle. Romy's professional career started off as a software developer, where he spent years as a Sr. Software Engineer working on AOL Instant Messenger. His transition into product management began with a focus on web, Mac, and mobile messaging.

Romy received his Bachelor of Science degree in Computer Science from George Mason University.

What does the term "product manager" mean to you?

Product management is about navigating teams to produce desired outcomes. In the most obvious case, the outcome is a tangible app or service that solves a problem for a specific customer. Day to day, outcomes are less obvious but ever present. Forming the right team for a project, being the dev-whisperer to gain engineering buy in, bringing in donuts for a software release, in all of these situations, the product manager is steering smaller outcomes that lead to larger ones.

How does the role of product manager differ between a startup and an established firm?

I know firsthand that in an established firm, it almost feels like you have unlimited resources.

In some of the larger organizations I worked at, I had it too good. If I had questions about how users interacted with our products, I could cobble up some bullet points and send them to the user research team. If I wasn't sure if a feature had legal implications, I'd shoot over an email to legal and they'd help figure it out. If I needed computers or software, I'd put a request in and they'd magically show up at my desk. And let's not get started on conferences, travel, and hotels.

When you're in a startup, you don't have these luxuries.

A user research team? Congratulations! You and your designers are now the user research team. Legal? Work with the legal consulting agency, but please get everything solved with minimal back and forth - time is literally money. Device goods? You either get a laptop or a desktop - not both. The conferences you attend better yield direct value and the hotels you stay at aren't "on the strip". In fact, if you can, stay with friends or family.

© Aswin Pranam 2018
A. Pranam, *Product Management Essentials*, https://doi.org/10.1007/978-1-4842-3303-0_21

How has your role changed as you've gone up the ranks to VP of Product? Can you describe your day-to-day?

Since I'm in a startup, some of my day-to-day activities haven't changed. I'm still an individual contributor for one of our products and I continue participating in stand-ups and retrospectives.

That said, some things have certainly changed. For one, I now manage the Creative Team. This means more 1:1s and meetings, but it also means more learning, greater empathy, and participating in more creative activities.

What is your biggest fear as a PM?

My biggest fear is failing my team or the customers. To keep myself from worrying, I often check my decisions against the company mission and my personal values. This way when I do fail, I know it's in good spirit and it's something I can learn from.

What is an underrated skill or quality of a world-class PM?

"Caring"

I mean this in a very general sense. A world-class product manager needs to care about their product and their customers. They need to care about how a meeting starts and how a meeting finishes. If there is a feature that involves a lot of cross-functionality support, they need to care that their product is being handed off properly between teams. In fact, they need to care so much so that they're almost playing "helicopter parent" at times. They need to care enough to weigh in, and care enough to let go.

What's your approach for crafting a product requirements document (PRD)?

It really depends on the audience and product.

A product launch normally requires a lot of cross-functional collaboration so I tend to use Product Briefs. A Product Brief is usually 1-4 pages and will cover: Description, Hypothesis, Goal, Competitive Analysis, Cost, KPIs, and what the product is NOT. Once I get business alignment, I use Keynote to dive deeper into product and experience requirements.

Audience matters, though. If I'm meeting with the leadership team and I have to go into pitch mode, I'll use Keynote. If it's a finance-heavy initiative, I'll use a Google Doc or Spreadsheet. And if it's going to be mostly product and design, I may actually use Sketch.

Index

© Aswin Pranam 2018
A. Pranam, *Product Management Essentials*, https://doi.org/10.1007/978-1-4842-3303-0

Get the eBook for only $5!

Why limit yourself?

With most of our titles available in both PDF and ePUB format, you can access your content wherever and however you wish—on your PC, phone, tablet, or reader.

Since you've purchased this print book, we are happy to offer you the eBook for just $5.

To learn more, go to http://www.apress.com/companion or contact support@apress.com.

Apress®

All Apress eBooks are subject to copyright. All rights are reserved by the Publisher, whether the whole or part of the material is concerned, specifically the rights of translation, reprinting, reuse of illustrations, recitation, broadcasting, reproduction on microfilms or in any other physical way, and transmission or information storage and retrieval, electronic adaptation, computer software, or by similar or dissimilar methodology now known or hereafter developed. Exempted from this legal reservation are brief excerpts in connection with reviews or scholarly analysis or material supplied specifically for the purpose of being entered and executed on a computer system, for exclusive use by the purchaser of the work. Duplication of this publication or parts thereof is permitted only under the provisions of the Copyright Law of the Publisher's location, in its current version, and permission for use must always be obtained from Springer. Permissions for use may be obtained through RightsLink at the Copyright Clearance Center. Violations are liable to prosecution under the respective Copyright Law.

Printed in the United States
by Bookmasters

Printed in the United States
By Bookmasters